Power Ties:
The International Student's
Guide to Finding a Job
in the United States

Power Ties:
The International Student's Guide to Finding a Job in the United States

Dan Beaudry

ISBN 978-0-557-09762-3

For Deb
Thank you

Author's Note

This book is written for all international students studying, or considering studying, in the United States who would like to know how to find a job in the U.S. after graduation. It is a book for MBA students, undergraduate students and any non-American aspiring to transition from an American university to the American workplace.

While a student's choice of school and degree will certainly influence his or her path to employment, international students from all schools and degree programs face a nearly universal set of challenges when looking for a job in the U.S. You'll find these challenges, and the ways to overcome them, explained in detail in this book. The answers are now in your hands.

Contents

Forward

Be courageous. I have seen many depressions in business. Always America has emerged from these stronger and more prosperous. Be brave as your fathers before you. Have faith! Go forward!
—THOMAS A. EDISON, American inventor

Toward the end of 2008, the U.S. government passed legislation greatly expanding its reach into the weakening American economy. As a result, the Troubled Assets Relief Program (or TARP) is now pouring large sums of public money into the struggling financial services industry in an attempt to keep it, and the institutions that depend on it, from failing. Aside from the obvious negative implications the weakened economy has had on hiring within the financial services industry, the new TARP legislation brings additional challenges for job-seeking international students. In order to sponsor H-1B visas, companies receiving TARP assistance must now comply with a number of additional regulations intended to protect employment opportunities for American workers.[1] Some people believe that the new requirements are so

---

[1] Technically speaking, no new regulations are being created. Companies receiving TARP money will now be considered "H-1B dependant employers," which is a category of companies whose workforce is at least 15 percent H-1B. Whether the companies have the 15 percent or not, they will be required to comply with several checks designed to protect American workers. Additionally, exemptions from these extra "H-1B dependent" requirements, which would normally apply, do not apply to TARP recipients. For details on the new rules go to www.uscis.gov.

onerous that these companies will no longer be willing to hire employees that need sponsored work authorization. Unfortunately, many of the financial institutions affected have been among the largest employers of international students in the United States.[2] So what does all this mean?

It means that U.S. career opportunities for international students are more difficult to find than they used to be. And it means that it is now more important than ever for international students to have a powerful job search strategy that they can begin to implement shortly after their arrival in the States. This book will provide you such a strategy.

Welcome to *Power Ties*.

---

[2] For a listing of the companies receiving TARP assistance, and for other information, see http://hosted.ap.org/specials/interactives/_business/bailout_tracker/ .

Preface

Desire is the starting point of all achievement, not a
hope, not a wish, but a keen pulsating desire which
transcends everything.
—NAPOLEON HILL, author of the classic book
Think and Grow Rich

Neil, an international student[3] I worked with several
years ago, would regularly complain that he never got
responses to the hundreds of applications he'd submitted
online for American jobs.[4] He resolved to send out more
résumés, and to follow them up with emails. Bulent,
another international student, sent an email to as many
of his school's alumni as he could find, mentioning that
he was looking for a job and requesting that they "let him
know" if there were any available. When he received very
little response, he concluded that either there weren't
any jobs, or the alumni weren't very loyal to his school.
Monica, a third international student long frustrated with
hearing from recruiters that they didn't sponsor U.S. work

---

[3] "International student" is a term commonly used in the U.S. to describe a student who is arriving from outside of the country to enroll in an American degree program, and who does not arrive in possession of full-time permanent U.S. work authorization.

[4] Student names have been changed.

visas, decided to begin every networking conversation by asking, "Do you sponsor?" She rarely got beyond this question, as it was often answered with a "no."

Neil, Bulent and Monica are not unique. Their challenges are common to almost all job-seeking international students, and their responses represent three widespread, yet highly *ineffective*, ways international students try to secure jobs in the United States.

If you are studying, or planning to study, in America, you should know what it takes to remain here as an employed professional—just in case you decide that the following rewards of U.S. employment are too attractive to ignore:

- Experience in the decision centers of some of the world's largest companies and most well-known brands
- Fluency with business English
- A more prestigious résumé
- A lucrative American salary

And the list continues. U.S. work experience is a coveted rite of passage in the global economy—particularly for the thousands of business students entering U.S. MBA programs. Standing between international students and these rewards is a U.S. work visa—the documentation that immigrants need for full-time, semi-permanent employment in the United States. With tightening U.S. borders and increasingly restrictive immigration policies, finding a company willing to "sponsor" a work visa can be a challenge.[5] Here's why:

- There are many international students with very similar qualifications competing for work visa sponsorship.
- Optional Practical Training (typically a 12-month period of work authorization available through the standard F-1 student visa), while useful for an internship, is generally regarded by employers as too short for full-time, permanent employment.
- Depending on their academic field, international students must compete with many job seekers who already have U.S. work authorization.
- Many companies have policies against sponsoring work visas.
- If an international student's English isn't very good, his or her qualifications almost don't matter.

Every year I see a new crop of students enter American schools with dreams of securing an American job, and every year these students begin their job searches chained to the same misimpressions that plagued the students before them. For example, every year international students are surprised to discover that most companies

[5] Companies wishing to hire someone who does not possess authorization for U.S. employment must "sponsor" the person they want to hire. This means that they participate in that person's work visa approval process with the government.

Let me take this early opportunity to note that I am not a lawyer. When relevant to the Power Ties strategy, this book includes some general information on work visas. But immigration is a complicated and ever-changing issue, and readers looking for details on immigration rules should consult an attorney.

in the U.S. are not eager to sponsor an H-1B visa (the most popular form of work authorization for recent international student graduates). Students spend hours applying for jobs on company web sites and commercial job boards and are very disappointed when they get no response. They fly around the country attending career fairs and are dismayed when the majority of company representatives they meet aren't interested in speaking with them about U.S. jobs. Every year international students are shocked to discover that many of the companies coming to recruit at their school's campus routinely screen them out. They become frustrated and sometimes bitter as they are continually denied access to jobs for which they are motivated and highly qualified—jobs for which they had expected to compete.

From my experience on all sides of the hiring process, I've seen this cycle of surprise and frustration repeated annually. I want the cycle to stop! You deserve a job, and you deserve to know how to get it. In the pages that follow, I'm going to show you how.

The truth behind the frustrations mentioned above is that, all other things being equal, most companies don't want to sponsor a work visa if they can avoid doing so.[6] Sponsoring costs a company money, it requires working

---

[6] Are there exceptions? As with most things in life, yes. Some companies publicly advertise their willingness to sponsor a visa, and you should include these companies in your job search if they interest you. However, how many other international students do you think are applying for these jobs? Quite a few, indeed.

with lawyers and the government (neither a pleasant prospect for employers), and it often involves wrestling with tight deadlines and complicated timing. But despite all this, you can secure almost any job, anywhere. Keep reading.

All other things being equal, employers will pass over your résumé in favor of a candidate with U.S. work authorization. *Therefore, the successful international job seeker works to ensure that all things are NOT equal.* The savvy job seeker realizes that landing a job means uncovering opportunities that others cannot or will not find, and then impressing decision makers by selling what no one else can—his or her personal credibility, likeability and helpfulness. Luckily for you, successful organizations will endure the inconvenience of sponsoring a work visa if there is a clear business reason to do so. Successful international student job seekers lever this fact by clearly demonstrating their business value to the right decision maker. Finding hidden jobs and presenting value to a decision maker are accomplished through building a strong support group of professional and personal allies— Power Ties.

Every year, it takes many frustrating months for international students to realize that *building professional connections is the most effective and only reliable way to secure work in the United States.* Unfortunately, countless students waste months mistakenly believing that their qualifications alone will get them a job. Eventually, painfully, some begin to comprehend the following truths:

- Jobs will materialize quickly if you can show a business person that you can solve his or her problems.
- You can't truly discover those problems unless you meet and get to know the business person.
- You won't be seen as the *solution* to those problems unless you've established credibility for yourself and articulated your value.

Once students understand and accept these truths, they are mentally prepared to implement the *Power Ties* system and capture the opportunities that emerge.

--

Your first question might naturally be, "Dan, how do you know this stuff, and why should I listen to you?" Good question. In short, I've built a career on finding jobs for people. After a few years of management consulting, I started on a career path that has taken me deep into the world of hiring. I've played the recruitment game from all positions: "headhunting" technology professionals for client companies, teaching MBA students how to find and win jobs, and leading the campus recruiting machine inside a major public corporation. Throughout, **I've**

met, counseled and recruited hundreds of job-seeking international students from all parts of the world. As the architect and director of the campus recruiting program for Monster.com, I've discussed job search strategies with international students at career fairs throughout the U.S. I've interviewed them, and I've hired them with H-1B sponsorship. As the Associate Director in the career development office at the Boston University School of Management, I constructed and delivered a seminar series on international student employment to educate foreign students on the U.S. job search. I also created individual job search plans for these students and coached them on selling their skills in the American labor market. Many of these students found meaningful employment in the U.S., and several have become my friends. All of this experience has made it quite clear to me that a shocking number of international students have a very poor understanding of how to find a job in the United States.

I now manage U.S. corporate sales for QS—an organization that promotes international mobility in education and career development through products such as The World MBA Tour, Global-Workplace.com, TopMBA.com and TopUniversities.com. Other than a three-year stint consulting for Towers Perrin, an international people-management consulting company, recruiting and education have consumed my entire working life. I want to share what I know with you so you don't need to waste your time repeating the mistakes of those who have come before you. Let me put you on the right path now so you can win a job early and enjoy the last months of your student experience without the stress of a job search.

--

In the 2007/2008 academic year, over 620,000 non-American students were enrolled in U.S. institutions of higher learning.[7] Perhaps you were one of these. Because you're reading this, I assume that you are at least considering the prospects of U.S. employment. Whether you have only begun to entertain getting a degree from an American school or are already in the midst of an intense U.S. job search, what you are about to read will make your life easier.

Maybe your friends have studied and worked in the U.S. Maybe you have friends who have tried to secure a job here and failed. Even students who come to the States with every intention of returning home after graduation find themselves drawn to American employment. It's quite possible that this will happen to you. I remember feeling the same attraction when I was a student in Paris. When I arrived, I had no intention of staying beyond six months, but by the fourth or fifth month I was ready to stay longer—and I wanted a job. Perhaps, if I'd had the job-search skills and knowledge then that I'm about to share with you, I might still be eating crêpes on the Champs Elysées.

---

[7] According to the Institute of International Education: http://opendoors.iienet-work.org/?p=131590

This short book (and the companion volumes soon to follow) is an international student's guide to navigating the U.S. job market. It will help you get on the right path early so that you don't waste time chasing remote possibilities or feel forced to accept a low-quality job because you can't find sponsorship for the one you really want.

Don't make the mistakes that thousands of others have. Your job search as an international student will be more complex in the U.S. than it would be in your own country, and it will be different from what your American classmates will experience. But don't worry—you have an experienced guide. I'm going to show you that you won't need to limit your job search to the few companies that openly welcome job applications from international students. Through reading this book, you'll find that a visa is attainable at almost any company. You will be in control of your job search, choosing the company and your role in it. By taking the time to read this book, you're already distinguishing yourself as someone who can take action to achieve. Your drive and boldness will make all the difference in your U.S. job search, just as it has so far in your career, in your education and in your life. Your time in the U.S. is limited. Make the most of it, and get your rewards.

In the chapters that follow, you'll discover a detailed analysis of how hiring works within American companies and what it will take for you to find a way in. You will discover that your path to success is through mobilizing people who care about you to act on your behalf. If you've spent time in your school's career services office, you've probably heard the word "networking" relentlessly trumpeted from every direction as the solution to all your job-search challenges. Most people I know don't really understand what networking means or how to do it. Some assume it means going up to people you don't know and asking for things. Others imagine it's making witty remarks at a cocktail reception or pretending to like people so you can get something from them. Many international students I've met over the years are uncomfortable with these (false!) conceptions of networking. And understandably so! Most reasonable people would agree that these activities are transparent at best, and manipulative at worst. Building Power Ties—the relationships that will lead you to your U.S. job—does not work this way, as you'll see.

Working a room and standing out in a crowd are both challenging and intimidating things to do. I'm going to show you a way to build Power Ties that is far less scary than those sorts of activities and much more effective. It's a system that the best American job seekers use, and it is a critical tool for those without full-time U.S. work authorization.

Here is what *Power Ties* covers:

- Why and how companies decide to sponsor work visas
- How to uncover jobs that others can't find
- How to determine, articulate and broadcast your value to a potential employer
- Why building Power Ties will help you
  - find a job
  - beat your competition
  - change careers
  - have an impact on others, and
  - accomplish almost anything else in your career

As I've said to countless international students throughout my career, if you don't have time to build Power Ties, *make* time. Stop searching the Internet to apply to jobs online. Stop working on your résumé. Stop writing cover letters. Stop studying as much! I'm not joking about this. You'll find that the quality of your job and the depth of your happiness depend much more on your relationships than your grades. If I'm a hiring manager, a person I know and like is always a more viable candidate than a stranger who makes no impression—regardless of grades (within reason, of course). In short, the techniques I'm going to show you in *Power Ties* will help make you liked and known. I'll demonstrate how to harness the support of other people, and make a positive impact in their lives as well. Is there anything more rewarding in life?

Power Ties are not just for the present. Once you get your U.S. job, what will you do? Stop building Power Ties? I hope not. Consider the following example:

I worked as a third-party recruiter (aka "headhunter") around the time of the dotcom recession in the United States. Just before the recession, there were huge amounts of technology professionals working with H-1B visas in my home city of Boston. Many of my corporate clients had been quite happy to sponsor work visas because of the acute shortage of technology professionals in Boston at the time. However, when venture capitalists started pulling their money out of unprofitable Internet start-up firms early in 2001, the economy began to weaken, companies started to close and the need for technology professionals began to plummet. Work visas disappeared and foreign workers were given a few weeks to either find another H-1B sponsor or leave the country. You wouldn't believe the number of calls I received from desperate people offering to do "anything" to land a job providing sponsorship.

Was I able to help these poor people? Unfortunately, not much. First of all, when someone approaches you with an offer to do "anything," it's tough to believe that he'll be able to do it well! And second, their requests came too late. I was busy helping people that I already knew and liked—the people who had invested time in getting to know me, and who I felt comfortable representing to clients.

When crisis strikes—and it will from time to time—you need a support group to rely on. Will you be someone with Power Ties already established and ready for mobilization, or will you need to start from scratch in the midst of adversity? Building Power Ties is a long-term career growth strategy, not just a job search technique.

We've all heard that success comes from preparation and hard work. What we haven't heard often enough is that both preparation and hard work can be made infinitely more effective through building quality relationships. Advance your career as you would manage a project at work; leverage the scale and efficiencies of motivated cooperation. With Power Ties, you'll motivate your supporters not with cash, but with the currency of goodwill. You're about to learn how to accumulate a sizable goodwill budget and how to turn it into the U.S. job of your dreams. And, beyond finding a job, if you end up enriching your whole life through what I'm about to teach you, all the better!

Now, let's go get that job.

Acknowledgements

I owe a debt of gratitude to Deb Sgambelluri for continually making the time to read, re-read, and edit this book over the past year and a half. Her overall encouragement and many suggestions on wording, content and tone have improved the final product immeasurably. My deep thanks also go out to Matthew Westbrook, Lisa Toby, Willa Smith, Pam Beaudry, Susan Peppercorn, Jeff Holcombe and Dave Fetherston for their interest in this book, their support and their many useful suggestions. Lastly, I'd like to thank my wife, Elena, whose encouragement, patience and love made this book possible. I'm lucky to have each of you in my life!

Chapter 1
The United States Hiring Culture

Far and away the best prize that life has to offer is the chance to work hard at work worth doing.
—THEODORE ROOSEVELT,
26th president of the United States

Welcome to the United States!

If this is your first time to the States, you're in for a great adventure. Much of the world's cultural diversity is melting away as we all become more familiar with each other—particularly in the realm of international business. But plenty of exciting variety remains, and you'll find a great deal of it in America's universities and workplaces. While we may all be moving toward becoming mono-cultural "earthlings," I estimate at least a handful of decades remain for us to savor the world's diversity. Your transition to living and studying in the U.S. won't feel as abrupt as it may have been for someone arriving from your country 50 years ago. But there are still plenty of things that might strike you as unusual—particularly the frequent co-existence of the extremes:

- The temperature in public buildings set at tropical heat in the winter and near-freezing temperatures in the summer—all measured in Fahrenheit, of course.

- Left-wing professors and right-wing talk radio show hosts both forecasting America's imminent demise.

- Credit cards can get you anything... except laundered clothing, a parking space and a phone call, for which quarters are the only acceptable currency.[8]

Yes, you'll need to strike a balance in the extreme environment of America, but I'm confident you'll find enough redeeming qualities here to make you consider staying after graduation. America is a fantastic place, loaded with energetic people and innovative ideas. Students come here to expand their visions, build momentum in their careers, and climb to new heights.

If working in the U.S. is part of your plan, then there's a particular aspect of American life that you'll need to become intimately familiar with—its *hiring culture*.

The culture of hiring in America

In the United States (as in most countries), hiring

---

[8] Yes, I'm exaggerating a bit on these—but not much. My wife (who's from Spain) helped with this list.

decisions emerge through an elaborate ritual of courtship that directs and constrains the way job candidates and employers engage each other. This process and the roles companies and candidates play constitute a culture, with its own language, hierarchy and standards of interaction. An important first step in figuring out how to get a job in the U.S. is to understand its hiring culture, because if you're going to play the game, you'll need to know the rules. And without some knowledge of the inner workings of the game and how its rules influence the players you'll encounter, it will be difficult to understand why the job search methods I will later reveal (which often *break* the rules) are so powerful.

In this chapter, and in the rest of this book, I'm going to share with you my perspective on how hiring happens in the United States. This perspective is based on 12 years of experience in corporate recruiting, campus recruiting and in the staffing industry. But although I've been immersed in the U.S. hiring culture for quite some time, please don't assume that by telling you about its rules, I'm going to advocate that you always follow them. Quite the contrary! As most leaders and high achievers know, there are times when being "counter-cultural" is the best path to distinguishing yourself and having success. Because I'm a disciple of this way of thinking, you'll find some rather radical opinions and suggestions in this book.[9] But

---

[9] Goethe said, "Whatever you can do, or dream you can do, begin it. Boldness has genius, power, and magic in it. Begin it now." You'll discover shortly, if you

first you need to know a few important things about how most people approach hiring. Then I'll show you how and when you should run counter to the culture to give yourself the best chance of getting the job you want.

I'll be the first to acknowledge that people get jobs in many different ways. In other words, there are countless possible paths to eventual employment, and if you stumble around long enough, fate can sometimes get you what you want. I've seen job offers extended without an interview, or *any* prior communication between candidate and hiring manager. I've seen companies recruit superstars away from their own key clients. And I've seen lucrative jobs fall into the laps of people who were neither seeking a job nor qualified for it!

The reality is that given enough time, any method of finding a job is possible.[10] Although you may have friends who have found jobs with minimal effort, resist the temptation to rely on luck. Serendipity is a wonderful thing, but top professionals don't wait for fate to direct their lives; they make things happen for themselves. That's what I want you to do, and I'm going to show you how. Your job search time in the States is short, and my

---

haven't already, that I like quotes. I'm one of those people who buys quote books and reads them for pleasure. If you have a favorite quote, email it to me at dan@powerties.net.

[10] And if you have an infinite number of monkeys poking keys on an infinite number of computer keyboards, it's likely that one of them will compose a Shakespearean sonnet, eventually. Again, I'm exaggerating here, but you get the point—you don't have infinite resources and limitless time.

task here is to set you on the path that gives you the *best* chance for success given your circumstances.

I will say at the outset that both the nature of the U.S. hiring culture and the counter-cultural activities I'll suggest may surprise you, as they have surprised many international students I've worked with. Some students have trouble accepting informed advice about U.S. hiring practices because it can contradict what they've experienced in their job searches at home. Sometimes international students convince themselves that they already know how best to find an American job, and they resist advice to try different things. These students generally haven't heard about the special challenges they will face finding a job in the United States; but this doesn't change the fact that they will need to face them.

Before you leap into your U.S. job search, open your mind to hearing what you don't expect, and console yourself with the knowledge that most American job seekers are as surprised by these revelations as you're likely to be. That's not because what I'm going to tell you isn't true— it's because it hasn't been publicized very much... yet.

Let's start on the path to success with an open mind and a willingness to take risks. The rewards will come.

The hiring game: who plays, why and how?

Many forces have shaped the U.S. hiring culture over time:

supply and demand, labor and management interaction, government regulation, and social trends, for example. Ultimately, these forces have created a forum for people to come together to negotiate their interests and derive value from associating with one another. A comprehensive analysis of the American hiring culture could fill a book many times the size of this one, so let's concentrate on a few key elements particularly relevant to you and the Power Ties system.

Employer = Buyer, Candidate = Seller

In the U.S., it is assumed that a hiring manager (or recruiter) is in a "buyer" position and therefore a position of power. This may be the same as in your home country. The person recruiting gets to choose the candidates he or she wants to speak with, dictates the steps required during the evaluation process, and ultimately selects the candidate to hire. This is why job seekers are coached to wear suits to interviews, to be prepared to answer challenging questions during the interviews, to send thank-you notes afterwards, and to embrace many other self-promotional techniques. Candidates are expected to sell themselves. The "employer-as-customer" culture of hiring has a long legacy in capitalism, and it is very slow to change. Even when market conditions suggest that the roles should be reversed (as they commonly do in the U.S.), it's quite rare to find a hiring manager preparing for an interview by dressing up, practicing to answer candidate questions, or sending a post-interview thank-you note—regardless of how urgently that manager needs to fill an open position, and regardless of how few good candidates there are to fill it.

Different players have different motivations

Let's look at four key players in the hiring culture and what their motivations are likely to be in attracting employees. What does each player stand to gain by bringing you into the company? Examining this is important because you need to know what motivates your buyer.

1. Companies/Upper Management

At the most basic level, companies hire to produce more of something. For-profit companies want to produce more revenue; non-profits want more measurable value for their constituents. Dynamic and ambitious organizations are designed to grow, and growth typically requires doing more things and having more people around to do them. To a senior executive at a for-profit company, you represent growth in revenue.

2. Hiring Managers

I'll be using the term "hiring managers" quite often in this book. They are typically the middle management of an organization: the directors, vice presidents, managers and department leaders who hire and manage people, and bear responsibility for their teams' production. They are the people who ultimately make decisions on who is hired onto their teams.

Like companies, managers also hire to achieve growth. But because they work more intimately with the people they hire, they are interested in additional factors. To managers, employees are a remedy to some sort of pain such as not enough time, or not enough expertise. Managers are given their objectives by upper management and are responsible for achieving them—with or without employees. Hiring people allows managers to share their burdens and achieve their goals.

3. Existing Employees (future colleagues)

Employees may also look at a new hire as a solution to pain—an extra hand who will lighten the workload of the rest of the team. Like managers, employees judge new hires based on competence and, like managers, they often have a voice in whether or not a candidate gets hired. But perhaps more acutely than managers, employees have a stake in making sure that a new hire is compatible with the personalities of the existing employees. Each employee carries his own ambitions and political baggage. Therefore, the motivations of existing employees in the hiring process are perhaps the most complex to deduce. Depending on the situation, a new employee could represent a savior, a threat or anything in between.

4. Human Resources (HR)

Among other things, HR performs an important recruiting support role within a company. HR department employees are the traditional company ambassadors to the labor market, and the custodians of the hiring system.

There's plenty of variety in how HR departments are structured and how they touch the recruiting process. Sometimes the recruiting function is part of HR, sometimes it's not. Sometimes HR gets very involved in recruiting, sometimes it doesn't. Most HR departments run recruiting for their company, and can be quite involved in attracting and acclimating incoming talent. However, HR's role in helping you get a job might be a little different than you think... Much more on this idea shortly.

Fairness

The U.S. hiring culture emphasizes fairness, diversity and equal opportunity. There is a great deal of regulation around maintaining an environment free from discrimination, and most companies take seriously their ability to document their fair hiring practices. As a result, American job seekers find themselves filling out many forms, slogging through opaque procedures and sometimes being asked to "voluntarily" provide their ethnicity and gender. For example, some companies have so standardized the process of applying to a position that they will not accept your résumé unless it comes through certain prescribed channels—namely, the company website. In these cases, all applicants must apply online regardless of how they came into contact with the company or how senior they are. The goal, of course, is to ensure and record that all applicants are treated and considered equally and fairly. The U.S. has quite a reputation for lawsuits against discriminatory hiring practices, and companies spend a great deal of resources trying to protect themselves.

Résumés and cover letters ("send me some information")[11]

As a student (particularly if you're an MBA student), you will be inundated with advice on how to craft a résumé. Your career services office will likely encourage you to adhere to a standard format, and spend a great deal of time coaching you on how best to present yourself on paper. Advice on the art of résumé creation is abundant and often contradictory. Suffice it to say that having a professional-looking résumé is important in the U.S. hiring culture (although not quite as important as some would have you believe). A résumé is still the job seeker's passport through the hiring journey. Creating it forces

---

[11] A common line used to avoid speaking with a salesperson is to say "send me some information." The implication is that the prospective buyer would like some time to read over and consider the value of the salesperson's offering. The reality is that it is unlikely the prospective buyer will even look at the material when it arrives, let alone give it careful consideration. Salespeople are coached to sell their products in person instead of relying on paper to do it for them. As a job seeker, you are selling yourself, and your résumé and cover letter are your "information." Is sending them to prospective employers the best approach? Much more on this idea later in the book...

the job seeker to consider his accomplishments and his potential value to an employer. In the U.S. hiring culture, a résumé typically travels through the Internet in the application process, guides interviewers in evaluating candidates and eventually becomes part of a hired candidate's employee file.

The debate on the usefulness of cover letters has staggered on through the years. Some bastions of the U.S. hiring culture insist that cover letters are critical in allowing a candidate to express intent. The cover letter, they say, looks forward, while the résumé can only reflect a candidate's past. However, I think cover letters are dying. Recruiters and hiring managers have seen too many of them that say nothing important, and they just don't have time to read them.[12]

The international student image

International students who have come before you have done much to shape how you are likely to be perceived by U.S. recruiters. Many have made a strong positive impression, tactfully selling and delivering the unique skills international students offer (which I will describe in detail in Chapter 7). But you should also be aware of some potential negative impressions of international students.

---

[12] If you are ever asked to provide a cover letter, it is essential that you address the specific position you are seeking. There is no greater waste of time than to read a "form" cover letter that is intended by its author to reach a general audience. If you're writing for everyone, you're writing for no one in particular. If you don't have the time to customize a cover letter, don't bother sending one.

Wanting to work in the U.S., and often needing a visa to do so (more on this in Chapter 5), some international students have made the mistake of appearing desperate to recruiters and hiring managers. Many have also visibly taken offense when encountering resistance from companies unwilling to sponsor work visas.

No one wants to hire a desperate or indignant candidate. And no hiring manager wants to feel put under pressure by a candidate. (Managers hire employees to *relieve* pressure, remember?) Unfortunately as a result, some recruiters assume that international students are demanding and awkward and therefore try to avoid them.[13] But don't worry, this reputation is by no means universal and can be overcome—and I'm going to show you how.

--

The above elements, and many others, combine to shape the U.S. hiring culture. I've highlighted the players, their motivations and their perceptions because they all play a part in the system I'm going to teach you for finding a job in the U.S. Each of the key points in this book will connect to at least one of these elements in some way. Once you immerse yourself in your job search, you'll encounter

---

[13] It's never fun when people make assumptions about who we are. However, there is opportunity in being mis-classified. If you can demonstrate that you are contrary to your reputation, you will stand out quickly and positively. For example, everyone loves the trustworthy salesperson, the ethical lawyer and the customer-focused government bureaucrat. I'm not suggesting that international students have a reputation as sinister as these popular pariahs, only that there is opportunity in running contrary to perception.

many more surprising components of the American hiring ritual. Take note of them as you continue on your journey. But always keep in mind that *the U.S. hiring culture did not evolve with international students in mind*. Your situation is different from the average American job seeker, and you'll need to do things a little differently to be successful.

Chapter 2
Being Counter-Cultural

Here in America we are descended in blood and in spirit
from revolutionists and rebels—men and women who
dare to dissent from accepted doctrine.
—DWIGHT D. EISENHOWER, 34th president of the United States

Although you've likely done your best to assimilate into
the American culture as a student, there are times when
it might be counterproductive to do so as a job seeker. Let
me remind you of the additional employment challenges
you're likely facing:

- You'll need work visa sponsorship.

- You'll be operating in a foreign culture and (perhaps)
  language.

- There could be preconceptions of you that you'll
  need to address.

- Your job-search timeline is limited by the duration
  of your student visa status.

Make no mistake; there are elements of the hiring culture that you will need to embrace. For example, you will almost always need to treat employers as potential buyers. This is consistent with what most of them will expect. However, you will need to sell yourself in ways that might be quite different from what you are used to in your own country. I've worked with many international students who have had a hard time re-framing the assumptions they've brought with them from their home country. For example, in the U.S. you will be expected to share and defend your opinions in class, promote yourself to potential employers and accept that having excellent grades will not guarantee you a good job. If these expectations are foreign to you, some level of discomfort is understandable. But you'll need to overcome it and recognize that finding the right U.S. job will require more than being smart. It will require that you interact with others to share your ideas, and to let them know who you are.

Students are also frequently plagued by stale advice from well-meaning advisors who, themselves, have been indoctrinated into hiring-culture obedience. Because international students are in unfamiliar surroundings, it's difficult for them to separate good advice from bad. They often make the mistake of embracing advice that is familiar and comfortable and rejecting advice that requires them to do something challenging. As you read the rest of this book and encounter suggestions that seem unfamiliar or make you uncomfortable, recognize your discomfort as a healthy step toward liberation from self-imposed limitations. Sustaining your comfort is *not* why you decided to study in a foreign country. You want to grow; don't hold yourself back by sticking with what's familiar. If you choose comfort over achievement now, will you be comfortable with that choice later?

We're going to get a U.S. job for you, and while we'll operate within strict moral and ethical boundaries without exception, we will shed the arbitrary limitations of the hiring culture when it makes sense to do so. Would you like a specific example of how you should behave contrary to the U.S. hiring culture? Here's a piece of advice that might make you uncomfortable. *Avoid the Human Resources department.*

Read on.

The role of Human Resources (... and why you should stay away)

The "high priests" of the hiring culture

If the system of hiring can be described as a culture, then it might be appropriate to refer to people in Human Resources as the culture's high priests. In large organizations, HR generally manages entry into the company through a ritualized and regulation-laden initiation process. Let's take a deeper look at HR and explore how it fits into recruiting and hiring.

Here is surprise number one: people in HR and recruiting[14] are very important to an organization, but they are the last people international students should speak to when hunting a job. Understanding this counter-intuitive point is critical to the rest of the *Power Ties* system, so let's begin with an exploration of the pressures that shape HR.

When you discover what HR is typically accountable for, you'll understand why preserving the hiring culture is so important to them and why it's designed to meet *their* needs more than yours. HR supports internal clients, mitigates risk, is sometimes at odds with hiring managers and can be one of the first parts of the business to suffer budget cuts when a company is under financial pressure.[15]

Ritual obedience

The Recruiting department, like HR in general, supports other departments within the company. Recruiters find and attract talent because the hiring managers they support either don't have the time or the expertise to do

---

[14] I'll refer to HR and recruiting interchangeably from here on out. As I mentioned in Chapter 1, this is not always an accurate thing to do. HR and recruiting can operate together, apart or in loose cooperation. But generally speaking, recruiting departments either fall directly under the jurisdiction of the HR department or embrace the same rules of operation.

[15] I have to confess that I envision my former colleagues in HR shaking their heads as I advocate circumventing their authority and thwarting the recruiting system they protect. Because I used to be part of the HR fraternity, part of me hopes my former colleagues don't read this book! I suspect, however, that most of them would grudgingly agree with me.

it themselves. Finding and attracting great talent is hard enough—it's scarce and expensive in a strong economy, and hard to discern from the mediocre masses in a slow economy—but finding and attracting talent the "right way" is a greater challenge still. For recruiters, the *means* of recruiting can be almost as important as the ends. This is because recruiters are not only accountable to the hiring managers they support. They also answer to the larger HR organization, which is very concerned with *how* things are done within the company. Consistently doing things the "right way" necessitates creating and enforcing "process"—the authoritarian root of the hiring culture.

If you've already spent some time looking for a job or an internship in the States, you've likely heard from some HR representative that you should "check out the website" and "apply online" instead of leaving a paper résumé, or "send an email to recruiting@xyzcompany.com and we'll keep your résumé on file," or maybe you've heard that your school isn't one of the company's "target schools."[16] All of these frustrating comments reflect HR's pre-occupation with process and organization.

---

[16] I've said all of these things myself while I was working in HR. Why? Because there were too many people (and international students) asking me for jobs. I knew I wouldn't remember them at the end of the day, and I wanted to keep them all in one place so I could check them out later. Also, I was required by compliance standards to direct all applicants online so everyone could be considered equally. Note that neither of these two reasons poses an opportunity for a job seeker to differentiate him or herself.

The non-profit world of HR

What does it mean to recruit the "right way?" The Recruiting department is tasked by HR and senior management with creating and enforcing policies that control costs, maintain compliance with outside regulations (e.g. the government) and generally mitigate the company's exposure to risk during the recruiting process. This is an important job. As mentioned previously in the section on fairness, the risks of being sued for unfair hiring practices are large and ever-present. The costs associated with making a bad hire are also significant.[17] Companies document their decision-making in order to control these risks/costs.

While useful in mitigating risk, policy enactment typically translates into extra steps of operation for all involved, such as making records, seeking approvals, being "fair" and doing any number of things often interpreted by hiring managers as a nuisance. Although they grudgingly acknowledge the necessity for rules and policies, many managers become exasperated when recruiters dictate what things "must" be done and what people "can't" do. To the revenue-generating, external-facing employee, HR often seems like an obstacle instead of the business partner it claims and genuinely tries to be.

---

[17] Human Resources departments continually fret over the costs of hiring the wrong person for the job—and rightly so. The costs are immense. Among other things, an ineffective hire costs the company dollars in training, administration, and lost production and opportunity. HR hates costs!

I know many business-minded recruiters who are committed to being facilitators and not obstacles to their internal clients. They truly want to be business partners, contribute to the company's growth and make life easier for the hiring managers they support. Most recruiters make a strong contribution to the recruiting process. And many are frustrated with the extra procedural burdens imposed by their own rules and regulations. But in the end, they are hamstrung by the parameters of the HR mission: to mitigate risk, maintain compliance with regulations and follow company policy.

Following HR process is the price hiring managers pay for the support they get from the Recruiting department. Let's explore why many of them have decided that the price is too high.

Rules vs. results

At times, a recruiter's own frustration with following and enforcing policy can undermine his or her credibility with hiring managers. After eternally fielding questions from colleagues, such as "Why do I have to fill out Form B even though I filled out the same information two pages earlier?" or "Why do I have to post this job for two weeks, if I already know who I'm going to hire?", some recruiters, perhaps forgivably, discard the lengthy explanations of why non-compliance with procedure jeopardizes the firm, and revert instead to the familiar and unassailable justification for all seemingly trivial rules:

"That's our policy." Less business-minded recruiters tend to employ this justification early and often. As important as compliance might be, and as well-reasoned as the recruiting policy might be, this explanation does little to win the hearts and minds of managers already under stress to accomplish their business goals. There is something about HR's regulatory nature and the way their rules are communicated that appears to hiring managers as an inability to appreciate the true pressures of business. Such a perception is often unfair, but nonetheless present.

I don't, however, think it's unfair to say that there are many people in HR who have never been in an external-facing role and have never experienced the pressures of market accountability. Without some appreciation for how the company makes money and the importance of maintaining balance between regulation and productivity, the process itself becomes the purpose. This is particularly true if HR comes to feel that its rules are the true source of its influence. Once recruiters come to believe that HR policies carry more clout than the recruiting team's impact on production, they are tempted to lean inordinately on policy to bolster their power. When policy usurps production as a means of exerting influence, rule-making can exceed its original purpose of mitigating the company's risk and become a political weapon. If this happens, hiring managers begin to explore alternatives to working with their out-of-touch HR colleagues. There is opportunity in this for you, as will be explained in Chapter 4.

Vulnerability

A lion's work hours are only when he's hungry; once he's
satisfied, the predator and prey live peacefully together
—CHUCK JONES, Warner Bros.
animation director of Bugs Bunny

It's worth looking at how HR is viewed by a company's
senior management. Despite the constant push of
some excellent HR people to win a permanent seat at
the strategic decision-making table (and some inroads
toward this goal have been made by more forward-
thinking organizations), HR is in a perpetual struggle to
justify itself. Although most senior executives will boldly
affirm that "the people" are the company's most critical
asset, when money is scarce, HR is too tempting a prey
for starving budget balancers to resist.

The life of an HR professional can be exhilarating. When
business is strong, companies depend on HR to attract and
retain their top talent. Management allocates a generous
budget for the development of competitive compensation
and benefits programs, employee engagement activities,
professional development, innovative recruiting tools,
and other programs designed to keep employees happy
and bring in more of them. HR people are showered with
resources and attention because management's biggest
fear is not being able to expand staff as fast as plans
require. While management trumpets "Our people are

our most important asset," it falls to HR to deliver on the promise.

However, the heady, big-budget days don't last. The American economy is volatile, and its companies' fortunes rise and fall with regularity. When the economy takes a downward turn, optimism, earnings and growth plans fade. Management tempers its confidence in the company's prospects, and its enthusiasm for investing in existing employees. Looking for resources to survive the weak economy, management also quickly remembers that it will get no direct revenue out of the Human Resources department. HR, like finance and facilities and marketing, is a support function and doesn't generate money for the firm. However, the money (finance), building (facilities) and products (marketing) can't take care of themselves without resources to keep things running. For better or worse, senior managers often assume that the company's employees (HR) can. When times are slow, you can't run the business without accounting or products, but training and recruiting appear far less critical. As a result, HR departments are generally the first to lose budget, staff and influence as management reverts to its default priority of driving sales instead of company picnics.

I mention all of this not to belittle Human Resources departments. They perform an important function. I've written this section so that you can recognize HR for what it generally is—an organization with a regulatory, highly cyclical and relatively light overall impact on business decisions, and with a reputation for valuing process over results.

Conclusion: The savvy international student job seeker avoids HR

Never allow a person to tell you no who doesn't have the power to say yes.
—ELEANOR ROOSEVELT, First Lady of the United States from 1933 to 1945

Perhaps you've experienced some of the things I mentioned above in your professional life. I touch on the nature of HR as a rules-making organization for these reasons:

- To show why the hiring culture is so sacred to them

- To suggest why they are often disinclined to take risks (such as sponsoring your work visa—which I'll discuss later)

- To show why they are afraid of people avoiding their policies, and how they enforce rules to bolster their authority

- To illustrate the limits of their power and ability to help you—they are *not* the final decision-makers in recruiting

- To illustrate why hiring managers (the true decision makers) are often inclined to avoid them

- To keep you from spending your time with them

As the traditional conduit for new employees entering an organization, the Recruiting department is the natural first target of international job seekers. *This is a mistake.* Because most recruiting departments are a component of Human Resources, they are constrained by HR's propensity to create, champion and enforce rules. These rules, and the Human Resources department, are often the biggest enemies of an international student looking for visa sponsorship.

Clara, from the Dominican Republic, was an MBA graduate and a member of a Latino professional organization that my wife belongs to. Clara worked tirelessly to find a position in the U.S. and gave my wife and me updates on her progress each time we met at an organization event. Her discouraging stories were fraught with frustrating encounters with HR: "you need to apply online," "we don't have any open positions," "we don't sponsor H-1B visas," "send us your résumé and we'll keep it on file in case something comes up." I encouraged her to stay away from HR, but it proved to be too foreign an idea for her to accept. Unfortunately, Clara didn't find a job in the States and had to go back to her country.

When you're looking for a job you should invest very

little, if any, time trying to connect with HR. In fact, in most cases, you should actively avoid any contact with them until the very last minute. Here's the secret: If you build strong Power Ties, HR will be calling *you* instead of the other way around.

As with virtually everything in life, there are, of course, exceptions. Approaching HR might make sense if

- You want a career in HR

- You already have a strong personal connection to someone in HR[18]

- You're only interested in *information* on a company's career opportunities

- You have a compelling reason to believe that HR in a particular company acts differently than I've outlined above

- All else fails

If none of these things apply, stay away!

Selling to your customer

I mentioned earlier that you should embrace one

---

[18] Having an existing personal relationship with someone in HR can be quite useful. HR tends to have a deep understanding of the personalities, relationships and dynamics within a company. Some HR professionals also have early access to company plans (such as expansion, new locations, etc.) that might be of interest to you. However, this information isn't made available to strangers.

important component of the U.S. hiring culture: treating yourself as the seller and the employer as your buyer. One of the first fundamental rules of selling is "always speak to the person with the power to buy." Your success depends on whether or not your audience can: 1) recognize your value as an employee and 2) decide to buy it. Many recruiters will be competent at the former (perhaps even better than the ultimate buyer!), but each of them is acting as an agent for the true decision-maker behind the scenes—the hiring manager.

Obviously, most hiring managers (your true buyers) prefer to fill their jobs as soon as possible with someone they can depend on, not just to get work done quickly, but also to minimize the amount of time wrestling with HR rules and inertia. The hiring manager is your true buyer because she and her team are the ones shouldering the undone work while the position remains open. She is the one most acutely aware of her business objectives and what a candidate must be able to do to help her accomplish them. As a support organization, HR may feel these pressures by proxy, but it has much less incentive and authority to hurry through, or bypass, the rules that might slow down the process.

A point worth making is that some recruiters, recognizing that they don't have the power to overrule company policies (such as not sponsoring work visas), would actually *prefer* that international students meet with hiring managers instead of HR. Recruiters want positions filled, and the prospect of having a powerful manager overrule policy to make a hire can be most welcome.

The point is that hiring managers have the biggest stake in hiring the best person quickly, and they have the power to decide who they hire. For these reasons, it is with hiring managers that you should spend your time. In the next chapter, we'll turn to the hiring manager's perspective, and explore the real need behind the hire. To do that, take a moment to stand in the shoes of a desperate manager—one with lots of work to do and not enough people to do it (just the sort you'd like to meet!).

Chapter 3
How Businesses Recruit People

I hire people brighter than me
and then I get out of their way.
—LEE IACOCCA, former CEO of Chrysler

Imagine yourself as the CEO

Assume for a moment that you own a boutique consulting business. Your company has been working lean for a year or two as you've tried to get the business up and running. However, you've recently helped a highly visible client successfully launch a new product and your name is starting to circulate at high levels. Now, your phone is ringing constantly, new projects are streaming in, and business is booming. You've got enough work for the next three years. Great! The problem is, short of working your small team 26 hours a day, there's no way you could hope to deliver quality on so many new contracts. Your "working lean" days are over. You need help, and you need it quickly. Every moment you delay equates to more work not getting done and more stress on your already overworked employees. And if you decline the new business, you forfeit the very opportunities you just earned with your successful product launch.

You're the boss (the hiring manager), and you're responsible for making sure the work gets done. So how are you going to find the help you need quickly and inexpensively? Let's take a look at your options. We'll start with some of the more recognized ways to fill jobs.

Your paths to finding employees

Print classified advertising: countdown to extinction

Hiring managers with grey hair might consider advertising in the same place they once looked for jobs themselves— the classified section of the local newspaper. After all, the newspapers are read by lots of people within commuting distance of your office, and your ad will appear in the context of the interesting and useful information the newspaper provides. Are newspaper classified ads an effective option for finding employees? Not quite. Here's why...

Classified advertising in print newspapers is dying in the United States; it's expensive, and no one reads it. Overall print newspaper sales have been weakening for quite awhile, and the classified recruitment advertising they contain is on a path to extinction.[19] Sales are plummeting. Aside from being static and boring, part of the problem

---

[19] http://www.ere.net/2009/06/24/is-print-recruitment-advertising-dead/

with print classified advertising is that no one can find it. Basic job listings are stuffed into a sea of small text and rendered almost invisible. If their department budgets are modest, hiring managers can forget about buying anything bigger or more eye-catching. Front page ad space in *The Boston Globe* "Money & Careers" section, for example, costs $16,300.[20] And are there any guarantees for purchasing this high-priced billboard? Negative. A print ad is not guaranteed to bring in the required candidates, nor is it even guaranteed to reach them. Ambitious, technologically savvy professionals (like you) are not likely to be scouring newspapers for their next bold career move. Posting an open position in the paper isn't the fastest, cheapest way to recruit a star.

Print media advertising is gasping for air because its classified product is being made obsolete by the Internet. In order to cope with their declining market share of recruitment advertising, the country's biggest newspapers have decided to partner with major Internet job boards (hotjobs.com, careerbuilder.com, monster.com, etc.).[21] So, as a hiring manager, should you buy a job posting on one of the Internet boards to fill your open role?

To post, or not to post?

Over the past 15 years, the web has revolutionized

---

[20] These are current rates as of this printing. https://bostonglobe.com/advertiser/mediakit/globe_rates.aspx?id=10724

[21] If you go to www.nytimes.com, you'll find Monster's logo. The two companies have been in partnership since 2007. Careerbuilder is actually owned by newspaper companies.

recruiting. It is cheaper, easier and more interactive than print. Job boards are still the primary player in today's Internet recruiting, and there are thousands of online job boards in the United States alone.[22] At the time of this book's publishing, a single job posting on monster.com (one of the biggest boards) costs $375 (with "bolding enhancement"). For that price, you get unlimited space for your job description, the click and scroll ease of the Internet, 60 days of live activity and organization tools to assist with candidate tracking and regulatory compliance. Is it any wonder that online postings revolutionized the staffing industry and all but replaced newspaper classified advertising?[23] In addition to the major U.S. job boards mentioned previously, an immense number of other websites offer job posting functionality: some in order to make money, others only to provide opportunity to their members. Posting a job is cheap, easy and has the potential to reach as broad an audience as you require.

Still, from a hiring manager's perspective, Internet job postings offer limited value. Why? Because many high quality professionals (job seekers) never see them. First of all, most Internet job seekers have experienced the

---

[22] To get an idea of the vast number of job boards available on the Internet, download a free copy of the AIRS Job Board and Recruiting Directory (http://www.airsdirectory.com/mc/forms_jobboard.guid).

[23] When I was working at Monster, I had a neighbor who sold classified advertising for The Boston Herald. He would often ask me how things were going at Monster. I could sense his desperate hope for our annihilation. Unfortunately for him, things didn't happen that way. Monster formed a partnership with The Boston Globe (the Herald's arch rival), and my neighbor's woes increased.

frustrating "application black hole" effect—the tendency for submitted résumés to generate absolutely no response at all from the posting company. You've experienced this. So have I, and so has everybody else. Sure, it's easy to apply from your computer at home, but once you submit your résumé, you have no idea what to do next, other than wait and hope. You don't know with whom you're communicating, if the person who posted the position is a recruiter or the hiring manager, if anyone at all will end up looking at your résumé, if you will ever hear back from anyone regarding your status, or even if the job really exists (many posted jobs don't!).[24]

From a job seeker's perspective, the nice thing about an online job search is that it is easy to conduct. Job seekers can sit at home in their pajamas, read job descriptions, and click "apply" whenever they want to. No communication with anyone, no concerns about personal hygiene, low effort, no risk.[25] However, there's a significant drawback

---

[24] No one knows exactly how many, but a significant number of jobs posted on the Internet don't really exist. How can this be? For one, many companies—particularly staffing agencies—will use a job posting as a tool to build a candidate pipeline for when they might need someone in the future. For example, if I'm in the staffing business and I place accountants with clients, I'm going to keep a posting up on the job boards for an accountant regardless of whether I have an open position to fill right now or not! Why? Because I need to have candidates ready when my clients need someone. I don't have time to start looking after my client calls with an order. If I do that, my competitor, who is pipelining with "prospecting" job postings, will fill the job before I have a chance. Is this ethical? In my opinion, no. Does it happen anyway? Yes.

[25] In fact, companies will often encourage a job seeker's sloth by explicitly indicating on the job posting that follow-up phone calls and other outreach are NOT welcome. "No phone calls please."

to this sort of convenience: the effort required of the recruiter/hiring manager is equally minimal. Recruiters sit at their computers, review a few résumés, and respond to whomever *they* want to. Do they want to respond to the people they aren't interested in interviewing? If you were one of them and you were busy, would you want to? Job boards are impersonal, and they put distance between managers and job seekers, allowing both to operate without accountability to each other. Job seekers can submit a résumé to any job they want (even if they aren't even remotely qualified), and hiring managers can respond when or if they feel like it. Not surprisingly, when applications number in the hundreds, they often don't feel like it.

From a manager's standpoint, a candidate's ease of application can be counterproductive. For every applicant who actually fits what the position calls for, there are often 5 – 10 who aren't even close, and who are obscuring the manager's path to a quick quality hire. I've worked on the employer side of a big job board like monster.com, and I've waded through the bulky nuisance of junk applications—hopefuls whose qualifications were laughably inappropriate and desperate job seekers who had applied to *all* the jobs posted—from Vice President of Sales to .NET Software Developer. Ridiculous! Internet postings have the potential to clutter a manager's view of the right candidates and generally are not the fastest way to zero in on quality.

There are few things more frustrating to job seekers then unanswered or unacknowledged résumé submissions. This is particularly true if the job seeker sees near-perfect alignment between his or her skills and the requirements publicized in the job description.[26] But Internet applications go unacknowledged every day. In addition, sending a résumé through a job board could stamp the job seeker's name on a junk mail marketing list or attract phone calls from organizations of dubious repute. These inconveniences tend to discourage the highest quality applicants from spending too much time on job boards (as they should discourage you!).

Stepping back into the shoes of the hiring manager, you've got to choose the most direct path to the best candidates for your open position. Your work is important, your clients are demanding, and you want a skillful and proactive professional at your side; ideally,

---

[26] "I'm perfect for this job! Why hasn't someone responded to my application?" How many times have you heard people say these words? This common frustration stems from the job seeker's naïve assumption that the description on the job board is an exact representation of what the hiring manager is really looking for. Not always true! In my time in recruiting, I've seen plenty of "placeholder" job descriptions posted on job boards that sometimes only remotely approximate the actual position being filled. Why does this happen? There are many possible scenarios. Here are a few. Sometimes recruiters can't get a hiring manager to spend the time to review and approve a job description, so they move forward with their best guess. Some job requisition software systems require an uploaded job description in order to begin the requisition approval process; and if a description is not ready, a "dummy" description is submitted just to keep things moving forward. Sometimes a hiring manager will change the position requirements after the job has been posted, and the posted description will be outdated. Now you know!

someone with enough confidence in his own professional network and abilities not to bother with the nuisances of job boards. Any clown can apply to a job online. As a hiring manager, you want to keep the clowns away. You want the candidate who doesn't need to tell the world, "I need a job!" by posting a résumé on a job board. You want the satisfaction and the extra value of finding the person that no one else can—the person who is perhaps *already* in a job somewhere and is so good at it that her present employer does everything he can to make sure she doesn't feel the need to put a résumé on a job board. You want to reach the *passive* job seeker—the candidate who might be quite interested in your open position, but who will need to be proactively *found*. [27]

Some managers like to pay for access to a résumé database. Searching through candidate profiles and contacting those people who are of Interest is more proactive that just posting a job, and managers can focus on attracting only those candidates that interest them. Generally, this is a

---

[27] Yes, I realize that you are not a passive candidate—you aren't yet happily working. But consider this: what methods do you think a hiring manager would use to reach a high-quality passive candidate? How can you position yourself to be found in this way? The answer to both questions is coming later, but here's a hint—it rhymes with "Flower Pies." As I'll explain in greater detail later on, you can boost how you are perceived by hiring managers by emulating some of the characteristics of passive job seekers.

As a separate point, job boards have been trying in vain to lure passive job seekers for quite some time. Employers continue to ask for this access. However, passive job seeker access is a difficult thing for internet recruiting companies to provide because people who are happily working don't see the need to upload résumés on job boards.

reasonably good solution. But what happens if the people managers need aren't in the database? Or, what happens if there are too many résumés in the database that fit a manager's requirements? If you're a manager, you'll need to invest time contacting your many candidates to figure out which ones are 1) still interested in considering a new position, 2) interested in your job specifically, and 3) truly a match for what you need.

Complicating matters, if your organization does business with the U.S. government, you will be required to handle your online recruiting in compliance with OFCCP (Office of Federal Contract Compliance Program) guidelines. These stringent regulations aim to reduce discrimination by requiring that firms doing business with the federal government adhere to a consistent methodology of reviewing candidates. As a hiring manager, you're very interested in preventing discrimination, but you're not particularly enthusiastic about following the laborious and seemingly futile procedural steps the government claims will prevent it.[28] But you'd rather follow them than risk being audited and fined if it turns out that you're not in compliance, so you spend the time to follow procedures.

---

[28] One organization for which I recruited required that we review 25 online résumés at a time. It didn't matter if the first five résumés we reviewed were a perfect fit for what we were looking for; HR (and government) policy demanded that I review the other twenty and make a note as to why each one wasn't a match. If I didn't find what I was looking for in the first 25, I was required to look at an additional set of 25, and so on. What a time-consuming nightmare! Such is the world of HR (and the government).

Finally, job board recruiting solutions may be relatively cheap, but there is no guarantee that you'll get any results for your money. You buy a job posting as you would buy an advertisement. You pay for space, not results. The same is true with resume database access. You pay for the right to take a look, regardless of whether you make a hire or not. If you're trying to hire someone with skills in high demand, you won't find many of them surfing job boards or sending updated information into a résumé database. They won't need to. Your competitors will be contacting these candidates directly, and trying to lure them away from their present employer. At the end of the day, posting a job on careerbuilder.com or other sites like it— or searching a commercial résumé database—can work, but as we've seen, this method of finding candidates has some significant drawbacks.[29]

Hire someone to hire someone

If you've got a number of positions to fill, you might consider hiring a recruiter. To tackle a quick growth spurt,

---

[29] Some of you may be asking "What about social networking sites?" At the moment, there's quite a lot of buzz in the recruitment world about the power of "social networking" websites (such as facebook, myspace, twitter, etc.), as tools to attract talent. There's also a great deal of debate about how effective these sites really are for tactical recruiting, and for how much longer they will be popular. Do users want to hear from companies while they're interacting online with their friends? Some survey data indicates no, but many companies are betting on yes.

My view is that there is some tactical recruiting value in social networking sites—particularly LinkedIn—but that their real value is in branding and building relationships—both very important long-term components of recruiting that will be addressed at length in this book!

you might employ a recruiter on a temporary contract rather than bear the expense of adding another full-time employee. A good contract recruiter can call into other companies to find and steal the sort of quality, passive candidates you're looking for. Once you've hired who you need, you say goodbye to your contract recruiter. Although cheaper than bringing on a full-time recruiter in the long run, good contract help is expensive. Quality contract recruiters—ones with an existing relevant network of contacts and who aren't afraid to cold call to grow it—can easily run over $50 per hour. And again, there aren't any guarantees on the number or quality of hires that your contractor will get you. You pay for time, not results.

"Ok," you say to yourself. "I'm going to pay for results. If I'm going to spend any money at all, I want to make sure I get the hire that I need." Welcome to the world of contingency recruitment. Let's check it out.

Hunting heads for money

Third-party recruiters, "headhunters" as they are affectionately called, are people who find employees for companies, for a fee. Headhunters working on a *contingency* basis get paid if their client company (you, the hiring manager) decides to hire someone they found. Pretty good deal, right? Typically, a contingency-based headhunter will receive a fee that is equivalent to 20-30% of the new hire's first-year salary. For example, a company would need to pay the headhunter $20-30k if it hired a person at a salary of $100k. But at least with a contingency recruiter you don't pay unless you hire someone. With "retained" headhunter searches—typically used to fill more senior-level roles—the headhunter is often paid a third of the fee at the start of the search that she keeps regardless of whether or not the client company hires one of her referrals. And that fee is a percentage of total compensation (base plus bonus) rather than just a percentage of salary. Recruiting agencies—retained or contingency—aren't cheap.

As a hiring manager, if you're working with a well-connected recruiting firm, you could see results very quickly. However, it's just as likely that you'll invest time with the recruiting firm haggling over price, arguing guarantee terms or sorting through unqualified candidates submitted to you by recruiters hoping they can win your business through providing volume rather than quality.

Do recruiting agencies work? Many hiring managers find one or two agencies that they love and rely on heavily. But it's likely that they find these one or two after spending a great deal of time wrestling with and fending off aggressive headhunters they'd prefer to avoid. The biggest drawback to using recruiting agencies is that they are very expensive. Compare the cost of a job posting (a few hundred dollars) to the cost of an agency fee (likely tens of thousands of dollars). A recruiter's value is a function of the quality of his or her contacts and ability to find the people who are hard to find.

Summary

So there it is—a (relatively) brief description of the options hiring managers have at their disposal to recruit a new star employee as quickly as possible. You're the manager; what are you going to choose? Each can work in the right circumstance, but there are powerful drawbacks to each as well. Feel like there's anything missing in the options I described? Is there a better way?

After reading through this list you might be asking why I haven't mentioned the most obvious way of filling an open position. If you're wondering how I could possibly assemble a list of ways to recruit and not mention the most effective solution available, you're well on your way to understanding the points I'll be making in the following chapters and the opportunity presented to you. The solution I've saved for last is the secret that's not a secret. Almost everyone acknowledges that this method is quietly thriving deep within the U.S. hiring culture, yet few people understand how to make it work for them. In the next chapter, I'm going to show you how to make this "secret" solution work for *you*.

Chapter 4
Referrals

When you say it about yourself, it's bragging. When someone else says it about you, it's proof.
—JEFFREY GITOMER, sales trainer and author

The "secret" solution

Hiring based on the trusted opinion of others is not just the oldest recruiting solution; it is still the best solution. Recall our discussion of a hiring manager's recruitment options in Chapter 3. It's logical (and correct) to assume that before a hiring manager invests any money, time or effort in one of the recruiting solutions I mentioned earlier, he will first make the small effort required to canvass the people he knows to find a new employee. Who does he know who might be able to fill the role? Who does he know who might know someone else?

The idea of leaning on your neighbors for help is intuitive for anyone who has been under pressure to make something happen quickly, and the champion recruiters of the world still draw their strength from a broad and deep pool of personal connections. Only *people* can respond to an exact question immediately, and only people are capable of caring whether or not you get what you need. Even though the world is flush with information, the *right* information from a trusted source is still hard to find. Despite the heap of electronic résumés, job postings and search-and-match technology on the Internet, finding the *right* employee is still a challenge, and managers look to people they trust for referrals.[30]

Therefore, a manager looking to hire someone quickly, cheaply and easily would start his recruiting process with a quick question to everyone within voice, phone or Internet network range: "Hey, everyone. Who do you know who can come in here and help us out with this project?" Asking around the office takes only as long as it took you to read the previous sentence and costs the hiring manager *nothing*. In fact, the hiring manager saves so much time and money by filling the job with one of his colleague's referrals that he may be grateful enough

---

[30] Enter LinkedIn, Facebook and the many other social networking websites—the new Internet resources for gathering the people you trust and maintaining relationships with them. Social networking sites have become very popular with people who recruit because they can amplify the power of what has always been a recruiter's preferred method of recruiting—getting referrals.
Keep in mind, however, that the technology itself is not what's important to the hiring manager. The trusted contacts are. Online networking tools tend to inspire a great deal of linking based on acquaintance (or something even more trivial), thereby diluting the power of the referrals they could generate. Referral-quality connections—whether maintained online or not—are best begun with meaningful face-to-face interaction. After all, when it comes to job referrals, being in someone's LinkedIn network means nothing unless that person knows you and is comfortable risking her reputation by referring you to a colleague (or a boss!).

to award a few thousand dollars to that colleague as a referral bonus.

Beyond being cheap and easy, an employee referral carries with it the implicit endorsement of the referrer; because who would compromise his own reputation by referring people he doesn't think are any good? Referral candidates can be generated with minimal investment, and they come with the backing of the person making the referral. Recall from our discussion of the American hiring culture that existing employees have a special stake in making sure that a new hire fits the team's "chemistry." Therefore any referrals coming from employees are particularly prized by hiring managers interested in hiring someone who will bond with the team.

Companies have long recognized the value of internal referrals, and they put resources behind exploiting that value. Many companies rely on employee referral bonus programs for the bulk of their hiring, and they encourage wide employee participation by publicizing their program as a second job within the company. "Augment your salary with referral bonuses" is their enticing message.[31]

---

[31] In the CareerXroads 8th Annual Source of Hire Study: What Happened in 2008 and What It Means for 2009, principals and recruitment experts Gerry Crispin and Mark Mehler find that 27 percent of all hires from companies surveyed came from referrals. They also find that an incredible 31 percent of respondents hired one out of every four referrals they received. They go on to say, "We continue to advise jobseekers to NEVER apply to a company without first networking to an employee in that firm for a referral. The difference in probability of getting 'up to bat' is too large to ignore." http://www.careerxroads.com/news/SourcesofHire09.pdf

The power of hiring through personal referrals is only "secret" to those who don't know much about how hiring really happens. Included in this group are technology/ Internet purists, people new to the job market (like students), and those under the delusion that hiring based on "who you know" is a thing of the past. If you think most hiring begins online, you've been watching too many monster.com commercials.

Referrals are profitable for everyone: The boss wants the referred candidate hired because he can avoid costs in time and money associated with the options noted in Chapter 3. The referring employee wants the referred candidate hired because she can make some money on a referral bonus and appear helpful, innovative and connected. And even the recruiter (if he has been involved) typically benefits because he gets credit (and likely bonus pay) for a filled job without having to do any work sourcing candidates.[32] It is an absolute win for everyone involved and an obvious opportunity for someone looking for work—like you.

What all of this means for you

We've just spent two and a half chapters laying groundwork—talking about how hiring works in the U.S., who does what, and why. What does all of this mean for you, the international student looking for a career in the

---

[32] This is assuming that the recruiter isn't forced by HR to oppose the hire because of a "no visa sponsorship" policy, in which case no one benefits.

U.S.? It means that if you're well qualified and you've met and impressed someone in the range of a hiring manager's personal connections (*before* he asks those connections for a referral), your dream job is likely yours.[33] You will enjoy the advantage of being personally endorsed by someone with clout, and you'll be in the running for a job for which very few others were considered or perhaps *even knew about*. What does that mean? Let me explain.

The 80 percent rule

It has become almost accepted dogma in the recruiting industry that 80 percent of all open positions are never publicized. Why? Because there's no need to pay to publicize a job when you can fill it through a referral for almost no cost. This means that 80 percent of the country's open jobs *never reach* the newspapers, online job boards, company websites or third-party recruiters mentioned in the previous chapter. Think about that for a moment. Did you realize that all the open jobs you've heard about in your career were only a fifth of the total pool? The other four-fifths constitute the "hidden job market," and you don't get access to them unless you're referred in. The recruiting industry—companies who make a living helping other companies find and hire

---

[33] Being well qualified is, of course, essential to this whole process; there is no legitimate substitute for being good at what you do. It is important to be able to perform the duties of the position with excellence, and to possess strong interviewing skills and professional acumen. All graduates going into the business world must have these two qualities as a baseline for success. If you need help with these things, set up a meeting with your career services office.

employees—handles only the leftovers: those jobs that can't be filled through referrals. The implications of the 80 percent rule may seem obvious, but let's be explicit. Why should you try to access the hidden job market? There are many reasons.

Access to more and better jobs

Obviously the more openings you know about, the more choice and opportunity there is for you in the market. And think about this: could it be that the ideal position for you is one that never gets advertised? Could it be that your dream job is so attractive that hiring managers can easily fill it by relying solely on their personal connections? How many job postings do you think there are for actors, for example, or business partners, or TV broadcasters? What about the perfect job for you that you don't even know exists?

Let's take this line of thought one step further. How many post-graduation career paths are you even aware of, and where did this awareness come from? Did it emerge from job postings you've seen—reflecting a mere 20 percent of the jobs in the market? In my experience, students have a surprisingly narrow view of what they want to do after graduation, and this is true for undergraduates and MBA students alike. Their impressions of what's available come from what campus recruiting departments have fed them, rather than their own reconnaissance. Don't misunderstand me; there are some great opportunities with companies that recruit on campus. But are you comfortable choosing a career path without at least some knowledge of the other 80 percent of jobs?

The hidden job market contains gems that are so popular there's no need to advertise them. That's why you need to make sure these jobs aren't hidden from *you*.

Less competition

The 20 percent of positions that are not hidden are, by definition, visible to everyone. These jobs can be found (and pursued) by anyone with an Internet connection, anyone in the vast databases of the world's staffing agencies, or anyone trying to contact HR. And how many graduates are there in the U.S. every year adopting these tactics? Too many. When you go to monster.com or work with a headhunter, you're competing with almost *everyone* else in the job market for *only 20 percent* of the total job pool. More applicants + fewer jobs = bad chances for you. But in the hidden job market, where jobs are more plentiful and competition is scarce, the math is firmly in your favor.

Inside advocacy

We'll be talking about this in greater detail in Chapter 7, but if you're starting to hear from people about jobs in the hidden market, it's because they are thinking about you. If people are thinking about you enough to bring a job to your attention, it's likely that they would be comfortable *recommending* you for the role as well. In the hidden job market, exclusive access and personal endorsement go hand in hand. Can you think of a more potent combination in a job search?

A chance to speak for yourself

Once a manager decides to publicize a job opening through the Internet (home of the "unhidden" and "leftover" job market), the recruiting process changes from a competition of candidates to a competition of résumés. As Internet users start clicking the "apply" button and the résumés start flooding in, two things happen. First, recruiters (HR) are likely to assume control over the hiring process from managers; and second, the recruiting approach changes from gathering candidates to screening them out.

In the sea of identical-looking applicant résumés, recruiters begin to look for any reason to make their pile of applications smaller. Did your spell-checker miss a "there" when you should have written "their"? You're gone. Is your "objective statement" not perfectly relevant to the job? Should you not have put in an "objective statement?" Or did you fail to include the exact key words the recruiter was looking for? In the trash. Are your action bullets not written in the third person? Goodbye. Do you need visa sponsorship? Over before it starts! You've just been reduced from a dynamic professional with energy and personality to a static piece of paper—just like all the rest of your competition. Your enthusiasm, verbal communication skills, problem-solving prowess and personality are no longer factors.

It's very much in your interest to be on a short list of *referred* applicants—not just because of the reduced competition but because having a small list of options makes hiring managers (and recruiters) less picky. They concentrate on the job's most important requirements and forget the trivia that might otherwise sway their decision when applications are plentiful. The contest for highly publicized jobs (i.e. Internet postings) is often unforgiving and unfair. Decisions hinge on résumé writing skills instead of job performance skills, and everyone has different standards when it comes to résumé etiquette.[34] Why play this game? Wouldn't you rather be one of the few focusing in on the hidden 80 percent, articulating your value in person, directly addressing any concerns a manager might have about your background, and showing the real you?

---

[34] Your school's career services office will likely request that you spend a lot of time crafting your résumé. Creating an effective résumé is part of what career counselors have been trained to teach, and they will be eager to share that information with you. Take their advice and create an effective résumé. But don't forget: you want to be in a position to speak for yourself, instead of through a piece of paper. You'll get greater returns on time invested in connecting with people out in the business world than on obsessing about résumé minutiae.

Sought-after status

If your next employer finds you instead of the other way around, you're likely to have increased leverage in securing the job and in negotiating terms should you receive an offer. People tend to be more impressed with things they choose than with what they are being sold. Hiring managers are, too. Position yourself to be chosen and you will enjoy opportunity and leverage.

Putting it all together

Hopefully, I've been able to excite you about the advantages of job seeking in the hidden job market. How do you get access? The method is simple but not easy. You need to expand your range of contacts so that the hidden job market can materialize for you. When a hiring manager in one of your target companies decides to fill a position, you want to be included in the first pool of candidates considered—the referred candidates. To be referred, you need to have already met and impressed someone within that hiring manager's circle of trusted associates. This is what building Power Ties is all about.

Your concerns

If you're like other international students I've worked with, you may not be completely convinced by what I've written so far. There may be some points on which you'll want to challenge me. Below, I address some of the common doubts that job seekers (both international and American) have voiced.

Doubt #1: Large firms, process and bureaucracy

"In your hiring example, you're talking about what happens in a small company," you say. "What about hiring practices in a large firm? Don't big companies have standardized recruiting procedures that would prevent someone from getting hired just by knowing the right person?"

Let me first mention that the larger firms are the ones with the best-developed employee referral programs. Second, while a large company may have an established and bureaucratic hiring process this is, in fact, even more of a reason to build Power Ties. The reason is because candidates aren't the only ones trying to avoid the company's bureaucracy. Keep reading.

I mentioned earlier the tension that can exist between hiring managers and HR. Very few hiring managers enjoy slogging through the bureaucratic swamp of required hiring procedure, such as generating job requisitions, getting approvals, and filling out paperwork. Most medium and large companies have a formalized process by which new hiring requisitions are opened. Even though a manager may have approval from her boss to hire someone, the recruiting and hiring isn't supposed to begin without justifying the costs and getting approvals from Finance and Human Resources. Let's look at two scenarios on how the hiring process might unfold. In both scenarios, Tanya (the hiring manager) and her boss agree that Tanya's team is overworked and needs to hire someone. And in both scenarios, they need to get Finance and HR approval. But, take a look at how the two paths can diverge. Notice how much the job seeker's positioning can influence events. Let's suppose you are a candidate for this open position.

Scenario A

1. Tanya knows she needs help, but she's not sure exactly how best to use a new hire, or how to describe the role so that it will attract the right person.

2. She asks her manager, and maybe the Human Resources department, for some sample job descriptions.

3. Using the descriptions as a guide, she outlines what the new hire will do, what unpleasant things will happen in her department if she doesn't hire someone, and how the role will be paid for.

4. She files a requisition for the new hire, including an optimistic estimation of when she needs someone to start (usually, yesterday).

5. Once the requisition is approved, HR gives it to a recruiter to fill. The recruiter (Eric) contacts Tanya,

and she educates him on the role and what sort of person she hopes to find.

6. Eric offers suggestions on what candidates Tanya might expect to find in the market and then publicizes the position through job postings and other methods.[35]

7. You apply for the job on careerbuilder.com and get a response three weeks later.

8. Although there are 47 applications for the job, many of which are from other international students, you have a résumé that was fortunate enough to share four key words with the job description. Eric's automatic filtering tool recognizes this match, and he sets up a phone screen with you and the 6 other people who passed the résumé screening technology.

9. Although you can tell from the phone interview that Eric doesn't really understand the job, he thinks you're a nice person (or what most interviewers euphemistically call "a good cultural fit"), and you're one of the lucky three to be brought in for a

---

[35] One of these other methods could be publicizing the job on the company's employee referral site. If you have a good relationship with someone at the company, you can likely skip all the steps that follow in this example and move on to a face-to-face interview. If the person who referred you is senior enough, you'll enter the interviewing process with even more advantage.

face-to-face interview with Tanya's team.[36]

10. After several tough rounds of interviewing, you come in second place to a candidate referred to Tanya by her boss, and who was fast-tracked through the process and gets the job.

Scenario B

1. You meet Tanya at a school alumni event and request an "informational interview."[37]

2. You and Tanya meet up for coffee before work. You ask her intelligent questions about her job, the challenges she's facing and what advice she would give to someone trying to build a career in her field. Through your astute questions and by sharing some of your own experiences, you impress her as someone who could ease her professional burdens.

3. Tanya creates a job description that fits you.

4. Tanya submits a job requisition asking for someone like you.

5. Tanya tells the recruiter to bring you in for

---

[36] It is typically in the phone-screen phase that a recruiter will ask if you are authorized for full-time employment in the U.S. If you're not, and the recruiter says authorization is required, the interview is over and so are your chances for this position.

[37] Are you wondering what an informational interview is and how it can help you? There's much more to come on the power of informational interviewing. It is an integral part of the Power Ties system.

interviews.

6. You interview with Tanya and her team—all of whom have been told beforehand by their boss (Tanya) how good you are.

7. You get the job.

It's obvious which scenario works best for you. Making the effort to get in early, impress Tanya as a professional, and have some thoughtful suggestions on how you might be useful to her will increase your chances of employment dramatically. Have I exaggerated a "worst case" example in Scenario A just to make a point? Not even close. Things could be (and often are) much more protracted and uncertain in a "Scenario A" job search than what I've just described. For example: 1) Eric may have 25 other open positions he's trying to fill for other managers, and Tanya's falls to the bottom of the list, 2) Tanya may decide to change the job description after it has been posted, restarting the whole process and leaving you completely unaware of the fact that the job you applied for on careerbuilder.com no longer exists, 3) Perhaps Tanya's position was filled a week ago, but Eric hasn't had time to remove the dead job posting before you see it, submit your resume... and wait.

These are just a few of the possibilities. And don't forget, in Scenario A, I made a bold assumption that you were selected to interview. When you rely on an Internet résumé to do your speaking for you, it's much more likely that one of the following things will happen, keeping you from getting an interview:

- You will be automatically blocked from applying for the job because you require visa sponsorship.

- Your résumé won't be noticed at all—either because it doesn't contain the words the recruiter is looking for, or it gets lost among all of the other résumés submitted for the job.

- The recruiter will screen you out in the phone interview because you require visa sponsorship.

- Your online application (speaking for you only as well as a piece of paper can) will go completely unanswered—read or unread!

Do all the problems I included in Scenario A (and in the list above) occur regularly and in the same job search? Yes they can, but even one of them can derail your chances of getting a job you really want. Most important, each obstacle makes the hiring process take longer. And the longer a job stays open, the more competition for the role will emerge, and the more likely unforeseen circumstances will ruin your chances.

You can circumvent a company's bureaucracy, streamline the interviewing and hiring process, showcase your value before being screened out for work authorization reasons, and cut out a great deal of competition by developing Power Ties and making Scenario B a reality. And the beautiful part of all of this is that most hiring managers would actually *prefer* that you do it this way! They don't want to wait for their job to get to the top of the recruiter's list. They want their role filled quickly by someone they know can do the work.

Doubt #2: Mandatory posting

"But don't large firms have a policy of posting ALL their open jobs to make sure they are conducting a fair job search?"

Some organizations (particularly government and academic institutions) have policies requiring even more delays before a hire can be made. For example, in the worthy name of creating equal opportunity, many organizations require that all open positions be made available to internal candidates first, and then posted for the general public for a set period of time before any hire can be made. However, the existence of these policies doesn't mean that hiring managers don't begin recruiting candidates well before the position is made available to the public. Hiring managers simply endure the waiting period—and perhaps conduct a few uninspired interviews—until they are allowed to officially hire the person they long ago selected (through building Power Ties!). In this scenario, the candidate search was over before it started. The winner was virtually selected before the first *official* interview because he or she pre-empted the process with an *informational* interview. And once again, the hiring manager is complicit in avoiding the bureaucracy. Hiring managers are less concerned with process than they are with getting their work done.

Doubt #3: No H-1B sponsorship

"But," you say, "what if this company doesn't sponsor H-1B visas?"

This is a crucial question, and one that has plagued many thousands of international students. We'll explore work authorization in depth in the next chapter, but here are some preliminary thoughts. A "no sponsorship" policy is typically something that a company (i.e., HR) enacts in order to:

- reduce the number of applicants to popular job postings,

- avoid the costs, delays and paperwork of sponsoring visas, or

- forgo the risk of your not winning the H-1B visa lottery[38] and needing to leave the country.

---

[38] The H-1B visa lottery is typically conducted in April of each year in the U.S. The U.S. government's fiscal year begins October 1. The number of H-1B petitions that can be approved in any given fiscal year is limited. H-1B petitions can be filed up to six months in advance (April 1 for an October 1 start date). In high-demand years, more petitions than H-1B numbers allocated for the entire year are filed in the first few days of April. When this happens, the government sets

In my opinion, each of these is a legitimate concern for companies—particularly the third, over which the company has no control. But it is possible for you to overcome each of them with knowledge, persistence and creativity. Building Power Ties is about using all three, as you'll see later. If you decide to build Power Ties after (or while) reading this book, you won't need to worry about whether a company has an official policy of sponsoring visas or not, because you're going to approach the company in an "unofficial" way. The traditional hiring-culture path to employment is through Human Resources. But, as I hope you understand at this point, you won't be speaking with Human Resources. You're going to connect with managers in your field—people who are doing what you want to be doing—who can recognize the value of your skills and decide that you're worth the risks of visa sponsorship. Hiring managers are the keepers of the hidden job market—it's their jobs that need to be filled. They care about results more than visas, and you'll get your best access to work sponsorship through them.

Take a look at www.myvisajobs.com for an irrefutable look at how many different companies have sponsored visas, big and small, all around the country, and across many industries. Interestingly, recruiters at many of these organizations regularly tell job seekers that their

---

a filing window, typically the first week in April. All H-1B cases received during that window are then subjected to a lottery. Then, only petitions selected in that lottery are considered for approval.

company doesn't sponsor visas. And perhaps that is their company's official policy. However, the data shown on myvisajobs.com is not a reflection of company policy. It is a reflection of reality.[39] Despite the fact that some of these organizations have strict policies to the contrary, someone within them has decided that the costs of sponsoring a visa are justified by the value of the hire. Keep in mind that companies don't sponsor visas out of altruism or "fairness." They sponsor because the cost/benefit analysis tips in their favor. It's your job to connect directly with hiring managers to make sure they have a full understanding of the potential benefit of investing in you.

Later in the book, we'll talk more about how to define and present your value. First, let's unravel the visa barrier. It is, after all, your primary obstacle to U.S. employment.

All job seekers—including Americans—would be well served by following the methods that I'm describing in this book. Anyone can benefit from building Power Ties, as I have in my own job searches. But the visa barrier is what complicates an international student's job search and what makes building Power Ties absolutely critical. Why do many U.S. companies have a policy against sponsoring work visas? How is it that many of these companies sponsor them nonetheless? And how can Power Ties help you make a sponsorship happen for yourself?

---

[39] Data on this site and others like it is based on information gathered from the U.S. Department of Labor.

Chapter 5
Work Authorization

If one does not know to which port one is sailing,
no wind is favorable.
—LUCIUS ANNAEUS SENECA,
Roman philosopher and statesman

The H-1B

Getting an H-1B visa will likely be your most formidable hurdle to U.S. employment and a source of stress, but it shouldn't paralyze your job search. Too many international students allow the visa barrier to sap their morale instead of motivate them to work harder. Ultimately, a motivated international job seeker can overcome the visa barrier through determination, resilience and executing an effective plan—and you can too. This chapter will explain why getting a visa can be a challenge and how this challenge can be overcome.

Taking control

Information is power, and having at your fingertips the

details of how U.S. work authorization is established will keep you in control of your job search. After building Power Ties, navigating the hidden job market, selling your merits and getting a job offer from an enthusiastic hiring manager, don't let it all fall apart because you're confused about how to get work authorization. What will you do when you tell your potential new boss that you need a work visa and he says, "What does that mean for me?"

An international student's first step in beginning a U.S. job search is to learn how employment visas work. If you aren't informed enough to explain in detail the rules of an H-1B visa and what an employer has to do to sponsor one for you, you're taking on several significant (and unnecessary) risks:

- The hiring manager will be scared away by the unfamiliarity of the sponsorship process.[40]

- You won't look like a prepared professional.

- The hiring manager will get information on sponsorship from some other source—one potentially unfriendly to visa sponsorship [hint: rhymes with "Truman Seahorses"].

---

[40] You could be tasked by your new employer with managing the visa sponsorship process for yourself. Many small firms have no experience with hiring foreign nationals and will depend on you to guide them through the process. If you can't do this (or if you sound like you can't do this when the topic arises), your manager's discomfort may block your path to a job.

Let me give you an example of this last item. In most medium-to-large firms, the manager will need to involve Human Resources to get you sponsored. You want the manager to be completely clear (if he isn't already) about what will be required of him and his company before he goes to HR. If the manager doesn't hear from you about how simple the process is—and it is relatively simple—it's possible he'll hear from HR that it's quite complicated. I don't think I need to mention that this would be bad for you! Knowing the visa process inside and out is another way that you'll be doing HR's job for them.

Take control! I recommend taking the following steps as soon as you arrive at your school's campus in the U.S.:

- Set up a meeting with an advisor from your school's international student office. Tell your advisor that you would like to stay in the U.S. to work after graduation. Ask what steps you need to take given your situation. Take notes on what the advisor says, including filing deadlines, lengths of eligibility and information you'll need to provide the government. Take your notes home and study them as you would any homework assignment.

- Spend some time studying the work visa information at www.uscis.gov—particularly the section on employment authorization. You might consider giving a small seminar on the topic to other international students. Practice articulating the details. Become known among your peers as an expert on visa sponsorship.

- Connect with a second-year MBA student (or a senior, if you're an undergrad) who is familiar with the work authorization process and may be going through it with a new employer. Find alumni from your school who were international students and ask them how the visa sponsorship process worked. What pitfalls were encountered? What steps would have made things easier?

  While in the first year of his MBA program, my friend Luis befriended a second-year student who had already been through the internship search and could describe in detail every step of the way. Both found visa sponsorship for full-time positions after graduation.

- If your career services office holds an event for international students, attend it!

A word of advice: It's about your career, not your visa

Decide what you want from your career, then you can assess what work authorization path will work with your goals. Don't be one of the many international students who gets this backwards. Your chosen career path should influence your work authorization options, not the other way around. Putting your visa first and your professional interests second will jeopardize your career and make hiring managers suspicious of your motives.

As soon as a manager senses that you're hunting a visa instead of a stimulating position on her team, your candidacy for the position is over. International students are notorious for having visa tunnel-vision. You'd be surprised how many of them have told me in interviews, "I just need a visa." (Thanks for being honest! Now I can remove you from consideration without another thought.) Orienting yourself "visa first" is bad enough. *Saying* it during a job interview is job-search suicide.

Believe me, I understand the temptation to take any job that will allow you to remain in the U.S. But the costs to your career and your integrity are too high. International students I've known over the years who have taken a job they weren't interested in just for the visa have not lasted long in their positions. They're unfulfilled, they feel unappreciated, and their managers are unsatisfied. Decide on a few preferred career directions that align with your genuine interests and then work on getting your visa.

To be clear, I'm not recommending that you reject anything but your absolute dream job. All job seekers need to make reasonable concessions to reach their goals, and you may need to be flexible on job description and timing to accommodate getting a work visa. But flexibility doesn't mean scrapping your dreams and blowing with the wind. Working in the U.S. is great, but it's not worth taking a job that leads nowhere. Begin your search with direction, in pursuit of a visa *and* a personally rewarding career. You can get both if you seek them in the right order.

Let me give you a quick overview of how the H-1B visa works. Although not the only option, it is the most common form of work authorization used by international students for full-time U.S. employment. Keep in mind that I'm not a lawyer, and if you're looking for legal advice on the H-1B, or any other work visa, you should consult one.

How the H-1B visa works

Once an employer decides to sponsor your visa, the actual mechanics of getting the H-1B are not particularly complicated or expensive. Basically, your sponsoring employer (or, more likely, the employer's lawyers) will need to prepare documents for the H-1B application and file them with the government. All in all, a company using outside legal counsel will pay roughly $5000 to $7000 to cover legal, filing and expedited processing fees. Under current rules, the visa application will be sent to the government and, if the initial demand for H-1B visas is greater than the number of H-1B approvals permitted in a fiscal year, entered into a lottery for one of the spots allowed by quota. Applications are accepted in early April, and the lottery winners are selected at random shortly thereafter.

In 2009, the quota of available H-1B's was 65,000.[41] For those with U.S. master's degrees, including MBAs, there were an additional 20,000 reserved spots available in a special "pre-lottery." The limits on the number of H-1B visas are set by federal law, and the speed with which the limit is reached (if it is reached at all) once the filing period opens in April can vary year to year depending on the demand for labor and the number of applications filed.

An application filed in the spring and accepted and approved as a lottery winner will become effective on October 1st. That's when the sponsored employee can begin work in H-1B status. The H-1B can be valid for up to three years and can be extended with the same or different employer(s) for up to a total of 6 years.[42] After 6 years, the sponsored employee will be required to either have a Green Card (or some other form of work authorization) or leave the country for at least one full year before returning to try for a third H-1B.[43]

Although this may sound a little complicated, the process

---

[41] Note that 6,800 of these are reserved for H-1B1s for nationals of Chile and Singapore. See below for more on H-1B1s.

[42] These extensions are exempt from future H-1B quota limitations.

[43] There are some specific exceptions to this rule that an immigration attorney can explain to you. For our purposes, let's secure the first sponsorship and you can worry about extending it later on.

can run rather smoothly—particularly if your sponsoring employer has an experienced attorney at hand. However, there are complications with H-1Bs that you need to know about, and we'll address them later in this chapter.

Know about your other options!

If you're not already hearing about H-1B visas from every corner of your career search experience, you will soon. The H-1B is certainly a common path to U.S. work authorization, but in your research you might discover another work authorization path that fits your ambitions and background. For example:

Do you know that students from Chile and Singapore are eligible for a special H-1B1 visa that sets aside 6,800 U.S. employment sponsorships exclusive to their countries?

Do you know that Australians are eligible to apply for one of 10,500 E-3 visas made available to people from that country?[44]

Do you know that H-1B visas for jobs within higher education or research organizations are outside the cap of 65,000?

Are you aware of the L-1 visa allowing a company to bring an employee to the U.S. after that employee spends at least a full year abroad working in a specialist or managerial position for an affiliate, parent or subsidiary

---

[44] Figures accurate as of November 14, 2008.

of a U.S.-based company?

Do you know about the TN visa allowing Mexican and Canadian nationals to work in the U.S. (in any of 63 specific occupations) for renewable three-year increments?

The point here is not to provide an exhaustive list of work visas, but to illustrate that there are several avenues to pursue and to motivate you to explore the various opportunities. Most students arrive without any idea how the U.S. work visa system operates. In fact, most *Americans* have no idea how the system works. But you MUST know. No one is as motivated as you to get accurate and precise answers about your future.

It's in your hands

Don't expect hiring managers to know about these programs. They don't! And even if they did and wanted to help you, they are restricted by United States law from asking you any questions about your nationality or origin prior to hire. If you can confidently and clearly present the steps required in sponsoring your work visa, you will alleviate your employer's reluctance to pursue it. And as I mentioned earlier, the hiring manager should hear from you how simple it is before she hears from HR about company policy. Doesn't it make sense that you advocate for your work visa as thoroughly as you would for your qualifications? Both are part of your package and part of what the employer will be paying for if you are hired.

A word about timing

One challenge in making this process successful is the timing. If you're studying in the United States on an F-1 visa, you will typically have access to limited work authorization called Optional Practical Training (OPT) and/or Curricular Practical Training (CPT). Generally, you will have 12 months of OPT and 8 months of CPT (if your school will provide you academic credit for work outside of the classroom). Many international students like to use their OPT for internships and other stints of employment while in the U.S. Doing so makes a lot of sense—internships can lead to great jobs. But be careful. If you win the lottery and you run out of OPT before the government issues the work visas in October, you'll be required to leave the country until then. Therefore, it's a good idea to keep a healthy portion of OPT reserved for the transition period from student to professional. If you don't win the H-1B lottery in your first attempt, a deep reserve of OPT can allow you to stay in the country to try the lottery the following year.

There's been a lot of talk in MBA career services and recruiting about recent legislation allowing F-1 visa holders to extend their OPT time if employed with a company that uses the U.S. federal government's "e-Verify" system.[45] However, this extension is limited to science,

---

[45] The e-Verify system is a government database that authenticates a candi-

technology, mathematics and engineering students and does not typically apply to MBA graduates. But if you're working on a degree in one of these areas, your OPT can be extended. Your future employer's lawyers and your school's international student office will be able to counsel you specifically on whether you qualify for the extension. Unfortunately for MBA students, most of them do not.

In any event, don't allow the mechanics of visa sponsorship to stand between you and your U.S. career. Answers on visa procedures are readily available on the government's immigration site (www.uscs.gov). Your biggest challenge, and the issue this book was written to tackle, is how to motivate an employer to hire you and agree to sponsor your work visa. Once you've secured these commitments, the rest of the visa process feels like spa treatment.

Why would a company not want to sponsor a work visa?

Why is visa sponsorship such a big deal for companies? International students have strong qualifications and a great deal of motivation. Shouldn't hiring the most qualified person for the job be an employer's highest priority? Obviously the situation isn't as simple as this. There are several common reasons why companies resist sponsoring visas. Here are some popular ones:

---

date's authorization to work in the United States. The U.S. government has been cracking down on companies hiring undocumented workers, and the e-Verify system is designed to stop the practice.

1. The company doesn't understand how the process works and is intimidated by the unfamiliarity.

I've mentioned this already. This sort of reluctance is typical of smaller firms that may not have been through the process of work visa sponsorship before. Or perhaps they've been through it before and weren't successful. In either case, navigating the unfamiliar and bureaucratic waters of the federal government can be daunting and, for some, thoroughly repellant. If you accumulate knowledge about how the process works, it will be quite useful in easing their fears.[46]

2. The company understands the process but wants to avoid the time and financial costs associated with sponsorship.

Although the mechanics of the H-1B sponsorship process are not particularly taxing, some firms still consider it an unnecessary expenditure of time and money. More work is more work, however small. And people naturally opt for the path of least resistance. A company's reluctance to sponsor you may be significant if they haven't already established contact with immigration attorneys. Your job in facing this challenge is to ensure that your

---

[46] As you speak to other international students and alumni, gather examples of successful sponsorship. Note the company name, the position and ideally the contact information of the hiring manager involved. This way, if you encounter a hiring manager in your own job search who is feeling uneasy about sponsorship, you can offer to connect him or her with a manager who has already been through the process successfully.

value is perceived as worth the effort required for your sponsorship.

3. The company doesn't want to hire someone who may be forced to leave his job (and the United States) if he doesn't win the visa lottery.

As noted earlier, there is a very real possibility that an H-1B visa request will be denied by the government. Generally, there are many more applications filed for H-1Bs than visas available.[47] A large number of applicants simply won't be lucky enough to win the lottery, and they'll be required to leave the country unless they have some other sort of authorization to remain (OPT, for example). Firms know that if their H-1B candidate doesn't win the lottery, and doesn't have enough OPT to stay in the U.S., they will either need to work out some sort of creative solution to keep the candidate on the books until the next lottery, or find another employee.[48] If you're the candidate, and

---

[47] This has been the case for many years, but 2009 has proven to be an exception. As a result of the softened economy and the new regulations on companies affected by TARP, the pace of H-1B visa application submissions has been much slower in 2009. And as of the second week of June 2009, the number of applications received was below the quota of available visas set by the U.S congress. Therefore, there was no lottery in 2009. However, once the limit is reached, all further H-1B petitions filed requesting start dates in the fiscal year will be rejected.

[48] These "creative solutions" often involve sending the candidate to a company office in the candidate's home country until a U.S. visa can be arranged. Although this can be a win-win solution, there are complications. For example, what if the company doesn't have operations in the candidate's home country? Or how does the company adjust salary payments so that they are appropriate for the candidate's home country? Many international students expect American salaries when living in places where the cost of living is much lower than in

you can't start working, the firm loses the productivity it was expecting from you and needs to dedicate more resources to finding an interim solution. Some companies are unwilling to accept this amount of risk.

The possibility of not winning the visa lottery (if a lottery is necessary) is a difficult barrier to overcome. Companies (including HR departments) would be more inclined to sponsor visas if the risk weren't so substantial. Unfortunately, other than being flexible with your geographical preferences and salary (in case the company needs to shift you back to your home country until the next lottery), there is very little you can do to mitigate this risk. Therefore, don't worry too much about it. Concentrate on getting a sponsorship commitment from an employer and then accommodate whatever creative arrangements need to be made to make the sponsorship happen.

4. The company believes it has an adequate supply of candidates for its open positions who already have full-time U.S. work authorization.

This is a common justification from some of the better-known employers, and you will find that many of the companies recruiting at your campus will take this position. Campus recruiters who receive hundreds of applications from U.S.-authorized candidates have little motivation to open their job postings to international students. They

the U.S. Companies are sometimes uncomfortable doing this.

just don't need—or want—more applicants. Rejecting non-authorized candidates (or screening them out of the application process altogether) is an effective way for HR to reduce their often overwhelming pile of applications. This is where accessing the hidden job market and targeting less well-branded employers becomes *key*. Stay away from Human Resources and campus recruiters. If you can become a candidate on a very short list in the hidden job market, you'll see the barrier above dissolve.

5. The company feels a duty to hire American workers for work in the U.S.

Immigration is a complex and polarizing issue in the U.S. While most in the business community embrace international employees as a key component to thriving in the global economy, there are strong sentiments in the U.S. that American workers should be filling American jobs. Nativist feelings could become more potent as jobs become scarcer in the U.S. Although you also may have strong feelings on this topic, my recommendation is to stay out of political discussions on U.S. immigration. Much as an invited guest would avoid commenting on the quality of his host's hospitality, it's best to avoid provoking conflict that could complicate your search.

--

These anti-visa forces are arrayed against you, and they are formidable. But fear not! The path to visa sponsorship is well-traveled (about 65,000 people a year successfully make the journey), and by reading this book, you are on your way as well. Visa sponsorships happen in the face of the stiffest resistance (remember myvisajobs.com from the previous chapter) and they can happen for you. Consider this...

While I was in career services at Boston University, a recruiter from MBNA (which is now part of Bank of America) told me that one of my students from India had no chance of getting a visa at his firm because "MBNA doesn't do that." A month later our student came to my office and told me he'd be starting there in June. He didn't get the job through campus recruiting, however. He got it from building Power Ties with the right people.

Why <u>will</u> a company decide to sponsor a work visa?

As we've done in previous chapters, let's assume the perspective of a hiring manager. Why would a manager decide to hire someone who requires visa sponsorship?

Let's be candid: employers don't sponsor a visa because they want to. They're friendly, decent people, but they don't care much about whether company visa policies are fair to international students or how badly you want U.S. work experience. They're interested in solving their *own* problems, and they'll sponsor a work visa only if doing so leads to a solution they need. Therefore, present yourself as an answer to a problem before you become associated with the administrative burdens of visa sponsorship.

When I was in HR, many international students I encountered at career fairs and on campus began their conversation with me by demanding "Do you sponsor international students?" When the answer was no, some would roll their eyes and make an indignant exit, or lecture me on how short-sighted our company was being. What a huge mistake—on multiple levels. First, the question itself has little value. If I'm working in HR and I tell you we don't sponsor, it doesn't mean you should stop considering my company (for all the reasons described earlier). If I'm a hiring manager, you haven't yet given me any incentive to confront company policy on your behalf. What's in it for me? Second, posing the question so early in the encounter suggests that you have a stronger interest in a visa sponsorship than you do in the company or in working for it. And third, expressing indignation is not a great way to build a relationship with someone at a company that interests you! [49]

---

[49] During recruitment events, I was actually grateful when someone would ask me this question because it gave me a quick way to reasonably end a conversation and move on to the next person in my long line of students. Don't hand someone (particularly someone in HR) a reason to remove you from consideration! From your perspective, finding out that a company doesn't officially sponsor visas is not a reason to cross it off your target list. Don't concern yourself with policy, until you've concerned yourself with relationships and your unique value.

While I understand the logic behind getting the visa question answered early so that you don't "waste time," the question comes from the mistaken assumption that company policy is the final word on visa sponsorship. It isn't.

Resist the temptation to get angry or show offense if you encounter a recruiter or hiring manager who tells you his company doesn't sponsor. Take the information as evidence that you haven't yet demonstrated that you're worth the effort required for sponsorship. Ask yourself this question: "Why should someone exert any extra effort for me without really knowing who I am and what I can offer?" If you can't find any compelling business reasons why someone would want you on her team, you've got more thinking to do.

Employers will sponsor you because you have something they want: talent. They sponsor you because they don't feel they can get what they need without doing so. Some progressive companies openly advertise their willingness to sponsor in order to attract the best people.[50] But most U.S. companies sponsor an H-1B visa only in the following instances of acute need:

- They are under intense time pressure to fill a job.

- They are having trouble finding skills they need

---

[50] As I mentioned earlier, you should obviously include these companies in your job search if they interest you. But I'm sure you can imagine what the competition is like for these positions among international students. And please, PLEASE! don't limit your job search to only these companies.

from U.S. work-authorized candidates. This includes (but isn't limited to) positions that require language skills, familiarity with a particular culture, and other qualifications that international students uniquely bring.

- Someone of influence within the company decides to make it happen for his or her own reasons.

It's difficult for you to have much influence in the first instance. You just need to be in the right place at the right time. Keep in mind that your chances of being "lucky" improve dramatically the more active you are in working the referral network. The second instance offers a bit more of a strategic opportunity. You can target firms that are likely to need the special professional skills and cultural familiarity you offer. But whether or not your targeted employers are having trouble finding those skills is still a matter of luck.

The third bullet point, however, presents a clear opportunity for you. Bullet point three can include any company, under almost any circumstances. It doesn't take time pressure or a skills shortage to get someone to want to hire you (although both certainly help). As a sharp and driven student with the resources of a university at your disposal, you are fully capable of identifying firms you would like to work for, and the people within those companies likely to be powerful enough to drive your H-

1B sponsorship.[51] You just need to know how to reach out to them, win them over, and rally them to your cause—in other words, how to build Power Ties.

How you can make it happen

What would cause a person of influence to become an ally of yours? You! You're going to impress upon that person that you are a solution to his problems. Identifying and connecting with powerful people *is* within your control and presents you, the international student, with your best chance to determine your destiny. Will you take advantage of it?

When a hiring manager really wants to hire someone, it's amazing how accommodating company policy can become. Here's an example. As a recruiter at Monster, I was part of the team that jumped into action when a stressed executive decided that she needed a particular candidate—despite that candidate's need for a work visa. All it took was that executive making a phone call to her assistant with the request to "make this sponsorship happen." Emails went out, names were mentioned, lawyers jumped into action, and it happened.

In my prior life as a headhunter, I completely avoided speaking with HR until my hiring manager client had already decided that he wanted to hire my candidate.

---

[51] How senior does someone need to be to have this power? Every company is different. My recommendation is to start with the most senior person you can.

Why? Because the client company's HR department always wanted to talk about policies first and my candidate second. And you can't drive an exception to policy (e.g. no visa sponsorship, headhunter fee limits, etc.) if you don't first have some leverage to make that exception worthwhile for the company. Your (and a headhunter's) leverage is your ability to solve a hiring manager's problems. Articulate this value to a hiring manager first. Once she comes to appreciate it and desire it, then watch HR policies melt before your eyes.

Conclusion

Some HR people will disapprove of what is written here— but I think those who are honest will agree that giving a hiring manager the candidate he needs is a recruiter's highest priority. HR is close to my heart: I was one of them, and count many of them as personal friends. But I've also been on the outside of HR looking in, and from that direction it doesn't look pretty for international students.

Having spent most of my career trying to evade HR, I experienced some acute moments of contradiction when I started working inside an HR department as a campus recruiter. I was a bit of a multiple-personality recruiter. While bound by my job to tell international students we didn't regularly sponsor work visas, I would simultaneously coach the impressive candidates on how they could "get around" me. If I had been in their shoes, I would have avoided campus recruiters like me, and that's what I want you to do! What did I tell them to do? The same thing I'm telling you now—connect with a hiring manager.

If someone from HR tells you his company doesn't sponsor work visas, you should politely thank him for his help and keep trying to connect with a manager. Do you think HR can appreciate your potential contributions to the company as deeply as a potential boss? Do you think most HR people feel empowered or inclined to overturn policy, the foundation of their authority, even if they did?

Does all of this mean that speaking with hiring managers *always* gets you a visa sponsorship? No. If you hear from a manager that he isn't allowed to sponsor an H-1B visa, there are three likely reasons why:

1. You've surprised the manager by asking about job opportunities and visa sponsorship too early— before you've conveyed your potential value through Power Ties. He feels pressure and is looking for an exit. HR's policy of not sponsoring visas is an easy escape hatch, and he will use it![52]

---

[52] As we'll discuss in much more detail in Chapter 6, asking a manager if he has any open positions before you effectively articulate your value is almost always counter-productive. Here's why: First, if you're effectively articulating your potential value to the manager, you won't need to ask about jobs. If there is one, and he thinks you're right for it, he'll want to tell you about it. Second, who cares if there are any currently open positions? If you present your value effectively, and the manager thinks he could use you, a position can often be created. This is how the hidden job market materializes, as we discussed in

2. The hiring manager has hiring needs but doesn't want you badly enough—perhaps because his need to hire isn't acute, or maybe you haven't impressed him.

3. The company has an iron-clad policy of not sponsoring work visas, and the manager is forced to obey. (This is not common, but it does happen.)

In any of these cases, keep in touch with the manager and move on to another one—preferably one more senior. You shouldn't remove a target company from your outreach list until you've heard from several managers that visa sponsorship is out of the question. This may suggest an inflexible company policy—and it is possible that you could encounter a company that won't budge.[53]

An H-1B is just an extra step—an annoying one, yes. But if you know how it works, talk to the right people and work

---

Chapter 4. Third, if you ask a hiring manager if he has any open positions prior to distinguishing yourself from "any other applicant," he's likely to direct you to the open positions that have already been posted on the website for... all the other applicants. Not only is this unhelpful to you (you could have found these jobs on the website on your own), but it blends you with the rest of the masses. If you seem like everybody else—someone looking for work, rather than some-one who can solve a hiring manager's problems—the manager will tell you to get in line with the other job seekers. You've been effectively dismissed, and it'll be harder to recapture the manager's attention to differentiate yourself. Always demonstrate value first! Much more on this later.

[53] It's important to make sure you're speaking with hiring managers who are senior enough to override policy before you abandon a company on your list. A policy that may seem insurmountable for someone at a supervisor level could be easily overcome by a vice president, for example. It's always a good idea to aim high.

hard, you will win. I know because I've seen the victories, and they are sweet.

Chapter 6
Power Ties!

The world can only be grasped by action, not by contemplation. The hand is the cutting edge of the mind.
—DIANE ARBUS, 20th century American photographer

Introduction

We now come to the brink of putting the Power Ties system to work for you. We've journeyed through the challenges international students face in finding U.S. employment. You've been introduced to the U.S hiring culture and seen that the hidden job market is ever-present and alive. You've learned why hiring managers go to the hidden market first to fill their positions, and how referrals power the entire system. You've seen that work sponsorships are achieved through meeting the interests of a prospective employer. Now you can see your opportunity. And now it's time for action!

Let's build Power Ties—the key relationships that fuel the referral process so critical to accessing the hidden job market. How will you infiltrate and navigate the referral networks that will lead you to your U.S. job and to visa sponsorship? How will you link yourself to people who are:

- decision makers,

- capable of appreciating your value, and

- able to direct you toward a job?

You're going to build Power Ties.

Power Ties (at last!)

Definition:

What are Power Ties, exactly? They are professional relationships that you as an international student purposefully build through strategic outreach. They are the bonds that give you access to the opportunities I've described in the previous chapters. They allow you to showcase your value and motivate someone to buy your talent.

If you've just arrived, it's likely that you have little or no connection with people in the U.S. professional world. If you're working on a master's degree, you're also very short on time. Your degree takes two or three years, most of which are filled with intense academic work taught in your second or third language. You've got a limited amount of time to purposefully construct, from scratch, professional relationships that will deliver value quickly and reliably.

Power Ties:

- Seek maximum impact in the shortest amount of time.

- Uncover career opportunities and position you to fill them.

- Capitalize on your status as a student.

- Are sufficiently deep for mutual benefit and can be easily deepened for a long-term business connection.

How will you build these relationships? Through two incredibly powerful mechanisms: one that's conceptual (networking) and one that is tactical (informational interviewing). If you can become skillful at both, you'll be a master builder of Power Ties.

Networking

It's possible that you've been hearing the word "networking" since the first days of orientation (if you've started school already). It was probably the first word out of the mouths of your career services counselors and now constitutes every third word they say. Listen to them. They know what they are talking about. If you haven't yet heard the word "networking" in the context of career development, you will—a lot.

Let's block out some of the noise, and take a moment to define networking. While you may be sick of hearing about it, the truth is that most international students I've met don't really understand what it means. Many of them think they do and are wrong. I've seen students mass-email their school's alumni database and call it networking. I've shuddered as I've watched students work a networking event by passing out their résumé and asking everyone they meet for a job. These methods are gorilla networking[54]—all muscle and no brain. Don't do these things! People will disagree on exactly what networking means, but most agree that good networking must be both personal and mutually beneficial—which mass emails and résumé distribution clearly are not.

Dictionary.com defines a network as "a supportive system of sharing information and services among individuals and groups having a common interest." I define networking a little more broadly. To me, networking is identical to making and keeping friends—with one small tweak. While friendships tend to occur by chance or circumstances, networking relationships tend to occur by design. The initial motivation to reach out is driven by a purpose other than the friendship for its own sake. In short, networking

---

[54] "Gorilla" should not be confused with "guerilla" – a term currently fashionable in describing intense, strategic and effective business methods (i.e. guerilla marketing, guerilla PR, etc.) There is nothing strategic about an 400-pound gorilla.

is looking for certain types of friends: ones who can be particularly helpful to you.

If this all seems like trivial semantics, it is! Just because networking is driven by a purpose other than the friendships themselves does not mean that networking friendships are fake, or any less valuable than friendships by circumstance. At the end of the day, it doesn't matter how your friends were made. But purposeful friendship-making (networking) will build you Power Ties the fastest.

The point of this section is that you will need to network to build Power Ties. And networking requires some effort and purpose to be most effective—both in beginning and sustaining relationships. The best networkers are pro-active in their outreach and extend to all members of their network the canon drivers of friendship: trust, open communication and respect. These are also the foundations of Power Ties.

"OK, so networking makes sense," you say. "And you've told me what I shouldn't do (don't be a gorilla). So how do I do this?" Great question! The answer is: informational interviews.

Don't hold yourself back

If I've done my job well, you're starting to see some opportunities for yourself—perhaps some very exciting opportunities that will separate you from the competition and win you a great job in the U.S. But along with that excitement, you're also starting to realize that uncovering these opportunities will require some action on your part—perhaps some action that will make you uncomfortable. If you're like other international students I've worked with, you may be in complete agreement with everything I've said, yet you're secretly hoping you can make all of this happen without having to do the active relationship-building part.

Let me acknowledge that American-style networking as a concept is foreign to many cultures. You may feel that conducting outreach to further your career is in fact *counter* to your culture. It's fine to feel this way. No one is going to ask you to forget your culture; go ahead and acknowledge the differences. Then ask yourself if you want a job in the U.S. and if you're willing to experience (or endure!) a different culture for a little while in order to get it. If the answer is yes, then put your old business culture on the shelf for a few months (along with any other excuses you may have), and go get your U.S. job.

Before we get into the specific tactics of establishing Power Ties, let me remind you of what you already know. Relationships drive everything. As a student, you've seen professors mathematically prove the efficiencies of teamwork, specialization and cooperation. As a professional, you've seen colleagues win promotions, investors and references because of the connections they've made. And from all the leadership literature, you've heard that you should find a mentor (or several) somehow. Throughout life you may have heard the well-worn phrase, "it's not what you know but who you know."[55] Given a lifetime of these messages, I'm willing to bet that you already believe in the importance of relationships in business and leadership. The only thing left to do is to create them. So let's do it.

Informational interviews – the silver bullet[56]

What are they?

In his book *Rogue Warrior*, former U.S. Navy SEAL and all-around tough-guy Richard Marcinko reveals the philosophy he adopted for enduring punishing military drill: "You don't have to like it; you just have to do it." While short on subtlety, there's plenty of truth in this statement. Sometimes when you're committed to achieving a goal, it's best to unburden yourself of the expectation that all the steps toward attaining it will be enjoyable. They usually aren't! For example, who really enjoys going through a traditional job search? Not many people actually take pleasure in writing and submitting résumés, answering difficult interview questions, being judged by strangers and risking rejection. However, people endure the punishing drill of the job search because they

---

[55] Sales guru Jeffrey Gitomer adds an interesting and quite accurate twist to this tired slogan. To him, "it's not who you know, it's who knows you." I might add to this that who LIKES you is equally important.

[56] A silver bullet is used to kill a werewolf. Informational interviews are used to kill the H-1B monster.

think they have to do it to get a job. They don't. There's a better way of getting in front of people who can hire you—and you might even like it.

As you might have anticipated, this better way is called "informational interviewing," and it's going to be your method of building Power Ties, accessing the hidden job market and securing a job in the U.S. True to its title, an informational interview is a meeting you initiate for the expressed purpose of gathering information. OK, nothing particularly revolutionary so far, but here's the beauty of informational interviewing in the context of a job search. There exist both overt and implied objectives with informational interviews; you want information (overt), but you also want to establish a connection with someone who might be able to help you get hired (implied). Here are your objectives in an informational interview:

1. To gather information from experts that you can use in your job search.

2. To showcase your talents and interests to a prospective buyer (or someone who is connected to a prospective buyer).

3. To create an opportunity for further meaningful communication *after* the interview so that a business relationship can be built.

While the information gathering is important, forming a strong connection with someone influential is paramount.

Informational interviews allow you to uncover what it takes to succeed in your chosen career AND build a referral network of Power Ties in your field. Both can be accomplished simultaneously. Here's how it works.

For an informational interview, you:

1. **Identify people who possess knowledge or experience that will help you in your career search *and* who could be in a position to hire you.** Their knowledge or experience could come from having worked in a profession or at a company you're considering. Find people who are doing what you want to be doing. Take time to develop a list of target contacts and companies that interest you, and to whom you think you can deliver value. And keep in mind that there are thousands of excellent companies you may not have heard of yet.[57] As we've seen from the 80 percent rule in Chapter 4, there is value in accessing opportunities that others don't know about. And everyone already knows about JP Morgan, Johnson & Johnson, Microsoft, P&G, etc. These are great companies, but big brand does not necessarily equal big opportunity—especially for international students. Be creative in devising a

---

[57] Your career services office will have plenty of resources to help you identify companies in the industries that interest you. You might also ask for recommendations of companies that have come to campus to recruit but who never seem to get enough applicants. These companies are likely to be happy to hear from someone from your school, and your career services people will embrace the opportunity to direct traffic to "under-served" recruiting clients.

target list and you will reduce your competition.

Find people whose backgrounds genuinely interest you, and the informational interview will be a pleasure for both you and your contact. Generally, international students are contact-poor in the U.S. How can you find the right people to interview? Sometimes the right people are a few layers deep in your network. Start with:

- Your friends and family (yes, family counts as part of your network!).

- Your school's alumni database.

- Your undergraduate school's alumni database (if it has one).

- Business networking web sites such as LinkedIn, Xing, etc.

- Your career services office.

- Contacts from prior employment or internships.

- Faculty contacts.

- Professional associations of people from your part of the world (there are many of these in the U.S.).

- Student organizations (particularly if you

volunteer to find speakers for your organization's events).

2. **Request a meeting at the convenience of your contact.** Don't be intimidated about reaching out to someone you don't know. It happens all the time in business, doesn't it? And people are quite pleased to be treated as experts. As intimidating as cold calling can be, it is my preferred method because it demonstrates a seriousness of purpose that email does not. It also shows that you are bold and driven—two valued characteristics in an employee. If you can't muster the courage to make the phone call, or if you have reason to believe that a call wouldn't be appropriate,[58] sending a personalized original email is an acceptable alternative. In either case, follow these steps:

- Identify yourself as a student.

- Say how you found the person's name (people are always curious about this).

- Say you're calling to gather expert advice.

- Ask for 15-20 minutes of the person's time for a face-to-face meeting—perhaps for coffee. (It's very difficult to turn down a request for so little

---

[58] An email is a poor substitute for a phone call. But I will send an email if 1) I can't get the person to pick up the phone when I call, 2) I think the person isn't often in the office, 3) I have reason to believe that the contact isn't the sort of person who likes being on the phone.

time. Your contact will likely stretch the meeting once you're in front of him anyway.)

3. **Prepare what your objectives are for the meeting (what you'd like to find out) and the questions you'll use to achieve them.** The best questions not only elicit the information you need, they also convey understanding and sophistication. Use your questions to position yourself as an insider and to demonstrate any expertise you may have that might be of interest to your contact. Be prepared to speak in depth about your own interests and strengths if your contact steers the conversation in that direction. Only you know the best questions to use in your field to serve these purposes. But here's an example question someone might pose to a communications professional in an informational interview. This question can be adapted easily to your area of expertise. In parenthesis, I've noted what's being accomplished by asking each particular portion of the question.

> "When I was running internal communications for XYZ Company (I've got work experience in your field), we wrestled with different ways to drive information to our employees and make sure they retained it (I've faced business issues relevant to your field and have tried creative solutions). In

particular, there were two approaches that we tried to balance—delivering information as early as possible, and delivering it 'just in time' for when our employees would need it and remember it (I've thought about subtle challenges in your field). As the Director of Investor Relations, have you encountered the tension between these two approaches? What ways of delivering communication to your constituents have been most effective (treating the person as an expert)?

4. **Take notes.** Record what you learn for later reference—it may be difficult to get in front of this person again. Write down any commitments you make to your contact, or any made to you. Taking notes also shows your contact that you value what he or she is saying (which is why you asked for the meeting in the first place), and will help you craft meaningful follow-up correspondence.

5. **Find areas of commonality.** Pay attention to what your contact tells you about his interests, or the challenges he's facing—professional or personal. For example, if he's an alumnus of your school and he tells you that he's having a hard time keeping connected, you have an opportunity to build a relationship by providing value. After your meeting, send him updates from campus

when something interesting happens. Small but thoughtful correspondence like this is effective in building rapport.

6. **If you feel like you've made a positive impression, end the meeting by asking whom else your contact might recommend you speak to.** Don't forget to do this! Have some ideas on who you'd most like to connect with so you can guide your contact as she considers how to help you. You will build your network most effectively through referrals. They will make your subsequent outreach calls warmer, put you in front of senior people you may not be able to reach on your own, and launch future meetings with instant common ground. [59]

7. **Keep the relationship alive.** Once the meeting ends, the hardest part is over, but there is much more to do. Certainly thank your contact with a note, but you should go beyond this. I've read countless "follow up" emails that have said nothing more substantial

---

[59] Many people make the mistake of asking the ineffective question: "Do you have any contacts for me?" When people ask me this, I have no idea how to help them. I know a lot of people. It would be much more useful to hear "Do you know anyone who works in product marketing at XYZ company?" for example. Bring your list of target companies to your meeting. Use it to prompt your contact on where you're particularly interested in getting referrals. Sometimes it's tough for a contact to pull names from thin air, and your target list will provide context and spark ideas.

In building Power Ties, you should try to do as much thinking as possible for your contact. If you make it very easy for someone to help you, you're likely to get what you need—and get it quickly.

than "I'm just writing to follow up." How dull! You need a more compelling reason for someone to pay attention to you. Find one. What immediate value can you add based on your meeting? Consider the challenges your contact shared with you. Did you make any commitments in your meeting that you need to follow through on? Did you think of someone your contact should meet? Did you do any more thinking about some of the issues you discussed? These are some things that are likely to engage people more effectively than the tired "follow-up" email. Whatever the nature of your follow-up correspondence, be sure that your tone projects a sense of *beginning* and not finality. This informational interview was only the first important step in building a strong Power Tie. The relationship isn't over!

Things to avoid

Now that you know how an informational interview works, let me tell you how it doesn't work. In an informational interview, you:

- **Don't ask for a job!** – An informational interview is for gathering information. While you'll also be leveraging the meeting as an opportunity to build a relationship, as soon as your contact feels that you're not really there for information, your credibility and the potential relationship are sunk. Don't be one of the international students who think they can build relationships by asking everyone they meet for a job. You'll annoy those who can most help you. Asking for help is an important part of networking, but you need to show yourself worthy of that help before most people will be inclined to give you much.[60] Ask too soon or too directly, and most people will avoid you.

When I was at Boston University, there were always a few students who would mass-email the school's alumni with their résumé. This high-volume, low-brain approach is akin to a charity spamming its most generous donors. Some resources are more valuable than others, and need to be handled intelligently to maximize what they can yield. Alumni have agreed to give time and advice to students (and they often give much more), making them one of your most valuable resources. The "find me a job" emails are destructive to the bonds alumni feel to their school, and the bond they are likely to feel with *you*.

International students that I've coached through this process have a very hard time not asking

---

[60] The next chapter will address how you can make it easy for people to want to help you.

for a job. It's at the top of their minds and they often can't get beyond it. What you need to realize is that the person you are speaking to in an informational interview *knows* you are looking for a job. It's obvious, isn't it? You're asking for advice on how to find a job. Do you think your contact is smart enough to figure out that you're in a job search? Of course! But the moment your questions change from gathering information to asking for a job, your contact will feel less like an expert and more like a sales prospect. After all, if you ask for a job and there aren't any, what then? From the contact's point of view, you could have gone to the website to explore jobs. What reason do you have for taking up your contact's time?

Information gathering, on the other hand, can happen whether a manager is hiring or not— and so can relationship building and referral making. This is why the conversation should be about advice only—unless your contact brings up your personal job search (and many will). But don't worry; they're smart enough to know you're looking for work!

- **Don't go in unprepared** – Prepare, prepare, prepare. Every business book in the world emphasizes the importance of preparation as if it were the most important aspect of any effort. Personally, I think people spend too much time preparing and not enough time taking action. Preparing is often much easier than *doing*, and it becomes an excuse to procrastinate. But consider this: In an informational interview, you've asked for your contact's time, therefore you've implied that it is valuable to you. Your contact feels important because you have requested his or her advice. Follow through on the good start you've created by coming to the meeting prepared with thoughtful questions to showcase your interest.

It's ok to use some "off the shelf" questions that you will find at your career services office or in a networking book. But it's best to bring questions that show some forethought on your part. Think about what is unique about your contact, and probe.

Finally, create some meeting objectives so that your conversation has some structure. Think about that uncomfortable silence that creeps into a conversation that has no direction. Adequate preparation will keep the information flowing and the impression positive.

- **Don't dominate the conversation** – You're there to listen, not talk. Remember, who's the expert? You might begin the interview with some information about you that will put your questions in context. And you should be prepared to answer questions about your experience and interests. But remember, the interview isn't about you.[61]

- **Don't hand out your résumé unless it's requested** – If I had a nickel for every unsolicited résumé that was passed into my hands by an overeager international student, I'd be able to fund a new library for your school. Pushing your résumé on someone is equivalent to asking for a job. Don't do it. BUT, make sure you bring a copy of your résumé to every informational interview. Many contacts will request it, and when they do, you should be ready. Let your contact determine when he's comfortable taking that step.

Why are informational interviews the preferred method of building Power Ties?

- **Easy access** – Perhaps the most difficult thing to accomplish in any outreach activity is getting people to set aside time to meet with you. The informational interviewing method lubricates this often slow-moving process because:

---

[61] Dale Carnegie—personal success coach extraordinaire—says, "You can close more business in two months by becoming interested in other people than you can in two years by trying to get other people interested in you."

o Students have access to many warm prospects through the school's alumni network.

o People want to help students.

o People are flattered by being treated as experts.

- **Subtlety** – A second challenge in networking is to request help without overburdening someone with your needs. The underlying strength of informational interviewing is that it communicates your need (a job) to the person you're speaking to without overtly placing any burdens upon that person to find you a job. Don't underestimate this subtlety. You're asking for information, not headhunting services; and while people will freely give advice, they'll quickly retreat when feeling pressure to provide you with a job. They don't know you yet! Informational interviewing keeps the pressure off and makes your contact more open to hearing about your interests and potential value as an employee.

- **Mutual benefit** – As I mentioned earlier, networking is most effective when it is personal and mutually beneficial. Informational interviews are both. Personal? The interview happens face to face (face time being a necessary component of any meaningful relationship). Mutually beneficial? The benefits to you are clear. Your contact's benefits may not be as obvious to you, but they could be substantial. In the next chapter, I'll talk in detail about the specific things you can offer. But generally speaking, by treating someone as an expert, you are fulfilling a basic need that all of us have to feel important.[62]

Nine reasons why an informational interview is better than a regular job interview

In the preceding chapters, I've spoken at length on some of the items below. But I think it's helpful to summarize how the informational interview leads you to strong Power Ties and the opportunities I've described. Informational interviews run counter to the traditional U.S. hiring culture, and deliver benefits to international students that they wouldn't get if they waited for regular job interviews. In an informational interview, you:

1. *Access the hidden job market* – The only way to find out about the 80 percent of unpublicized positions is from inside the company, and the traditional hiring culture gives you no way in. Informational interviews create a low-pressure access point that

---

[62] You might be tempted to dismiss the value of this potential benefit. Don't. Dale Carnegie puts "the desire to be important" alongside food and sex as fundamental human needs.

is consistent with the "educational" orientation of a student.

2. *Create your own position* – Regular interviews don't happen for positions that don't exist yet. But informational interviews often inspire a hiring manager to hire the informational interviewer.

3. *Reduce stress* – In a regular interview, the burden is on the candidate to demonstrate why he would be a good fit for an open position. In an informational interview, you are the interviewer, and while you still want to demonstrate your skills, there's no expectation that you will do so; after all, you're there to gather information.

4. *Sidestep job qualifications* – Unlike in a standard job interview, you have not formally given your consent to be "evaluated." Your reason for speaking with a hiring manager isn't that you believe yourself to be qualified for a particular job (even though you might), only that you're looking for information. To get the meeting, you have no qualifications to meet and no screening process to pass.

5. *Make the interview happen* – YOU decide when, where and with whom you will have an informational interview; not the company.[63] You're not going to

---

[63] Of course you'll need to accommodate the schedule of the person you're reaching out to. And of course there is the possibility that the person you'd like to speak with will decline. My point is that you control the initiative, and therefore dictate the "rules" and format.

wait to be chosen for an interview. You're going to make it happen yourself.

6. *Control the agenda* – If you initiate the informational interview, there is no set of job requirements to constrain your conversation (no job was discussed) and no résumé to have to defend (unless you decide to reveal it). The interview questions come from you, and as most sales books will tell you, the person who asks the questions controls the conversation.

7. *Avoid Human Resources* – No more need be said.

8. *Control the follow-up* – Because you're not an official candidate for a role, there is no company process or "required next steps" that constrain how you communicate with your contact after the initial meeting. You can follow the rules that suit your purposes.

9. *Shape the job* – Through informational interviewing and the subsequent follow-up, you have a chance to present yourself to a hiring manager as a solution to a problem. By dangling the carrot, you might find the hiring manager writing a job description for a candidate that looks a lot like you.

Power Ties rewards

Advocates

The most important rewards from Power Ties are the advocates you'll win. Strong advocates will think of you when the time is right. They will introduce you to others who can help you. They will vouch for you and bolster your credibility when you need a reference. In business, advocates are the most important asset anyone can have.

Differentiation

International students are always looking for ways to differentiate themselves. You will stand out by doing things that other people are unwilling to do. Informational interviewing, an intimidating task at first—especially for international students entering the U.S. business world for the first time—is such an activity. Do what others can't (or are afraid to) do, and you will be rewarded. This is true throughout business and often throughout life.

Motivation

The beauty of building Power Ties is that their power to make positive things happen, once tasted, is addicting. Once the initial fear and inertia are overcome, building Power Ties is a self-fueling activity. After a few meetings, you'll realize that many of the boundaries you've been observing your whole life are artificial. Imagine your confidence when you realize you can ask literally anyone in the world for an informational interview. I worked with a student who asked the CEO of Motorola for an informational interview and *got it*. Bold action is powerful, and this student felt its immediate rewards. Do you think his success in securing this meeting motivated him to initiate more of them? Do you think arranging informational interviews with other people got easier after that? You can be sure the answer is yes on both counts.

Will contacts always say yes to requests for informational interviews? No. Will you have to learn how to handle rejection? Yes. But there will be enough yeses to your requests to provide you with the Power Ties you need. And the few nos you encounter will reinforce how exciting the yeses are.

I don't want to sound overly dramatic here, but I believe that becoming comfortable with informational interviewing and building Power Ties leads a person on a path to freedom and empowerment. It takes the sting out of what everyone fears most—rejection. Once you've looked rejection in the face and learned to smile back at it, you're unstoppable.

Business skills

To build Power Ties, you will need to cold call, start conversations with people you don't know, ask people for help, creatively solve problems and develop a strong sense of how you can help other people. This may sound intimidating, but all of these competencies have broad application in the professional world. All successful leaders must do these things. So master them now on your own terms instead of later when you're under pressure from a boss. Building Power Ties is not only about winning advocates, but about developing skills that will give you an edge over other people too afraid to learn them. Get the skills advantage you need to continually win and keep the jobs you want throughout your career.

Career security

The bonds of loyalty that used to exist between company and employee are no longer powerful. Neither party feels that the other will be there when times are tough. There is very little that employees can do these days to create security for themselves in any one position. However, career security (and opportunity) can be created through the development of Power Ties. When you find yourself without a job, your network—a collection of advocates familiar with you and your potential—will open your path back into the workforce.

Clients and suppliers

Your Power Ties support network, if well tended, can become your client, or supplier, base. People do business with those they know and trust.[64] If you have business development or sales ambitions, the Power Ties you build in your job search will deliver value many times over— well after you get the job you want.

Summary

Let me summarize the Power Ties strategy so far: Informational interviews will provide you an opportunity to build Power Ties with professionals who can appreciate your value and provide you access to the enormous hidden job market. Remember that Power Ties are formed through personal and mutually beneficial contact. The informational interview is the face-to-face technique that gives you a chance to demonstrate your interests and value to someone who can both appreciate them and move you closer to a job.

In the next chapter, we'll talk about how to initiate and cement meaningful relationships through creating mutual benefit for you and your contact. What does it take to be memorable? What do you think you have to offer? Many international students I've met don't think they have much. How wrong they are! Let's uncover your value and leverage it to make sure that players in the hidden job market are thinking of you when the right opportunity materializes.

---

[64] Sales guru Jeffrey Gitomer says, "All things being equal, people will buy from their friends. All things not being quite equal, people will still buy from their friends."

Chapter 7
Your Value

The most important single central fact about a free market is that no exchange takes place unless both parties benefit.
—MILTON FRIEDMAN, American economist

Give someone a reason to care

Let's face it; there is a ridiculous amount of information in the world.[65] And much of it is being thrown at us by people who want something from us. Our email inboxes are overflowing with spam, our desks are piled high with mail from organizations we've never heard of, and our Internet surfing is choked with pop-ups. We didn't ask for this information, we don't want it and we spend money trying to keep it away.[66] We want less information

---

[65] Take a look at this website for some fascinating estimates on the numbers of bytes of information there are in the world. In summary, there's a lot. http://www.corporatesoftwaretraining.com/HowManyBytes.htm. University of California at Berkeley professors made the following estimates on how much information exists and how rapidly it is growing. http://www2.sims.berkeley.edu/research/projects/how-much-info-2003/execsum.htm. This 2003 study is currently being updated by professors at Berkeley, MIT and others.

[66] Consider the devices that exist in our world designed to manage our intake of information and keep unwanted information away. In the U.S. there are many

in our lives so that we can make sure we don't miss the information we really *care* about.

Although each of us wades through a flood of information virtually every day of our lives, what do we mysteriously revert to producing when we become job seekers? Information! Résumés, cover letters, elevator pitches, long-winded monologues at career fairs—all about us and why we're special. And then we distribute this information to as many people as we can—most of whom we don't know at all.

Once we need something from someone else (a job), we somehow forget that the only information that gets through a person's filter is information he or she cares about. Think back to earlier job searches you may have experienced; how much of your time was spent assembling and distributing information about yourself versus investing in giving someone a compelling reason to consider it? Every company distributing junk mail is as excited about its product as you are about your professional qualifications. Unfortunately, no one *receiving* this information cares! Without actively giving someone a reason to care about you, all you can do is hope; and hoping isn't a powerful strategy for making things happen.

---

examples: the national "do not call" list, pop-up blocker software, self-help books proclaiming "Take Back Your Life" or "Don't Sweat the Small Stuff," call screeners, spam filters, voicemail, caller ID, résumé screening software, general email inboxes such as careers@xyzcompany.com (ah, does this one seem familiar?), and the list goes on...

So how can you motivate someone to care about you? You already know the answer to this question, but for some reason you thought it didn't apply in the professional world. You thought that business was about data, cold analysis and dispassionate decision making. "Business isn't about caring, it's about profit." Not so! (Particularly not so with regard to hiring.) What you already know—and what applies to business relationships as much as anywhere else—is that people care about you when you care about *them*. This simple truth will be the subject of this chapter, and the eagerness with which you embrace it will determine the strength of your Power Ties.

Giving: The secret to all relationship building

When I was in career services at Boston University, I worked with Deep, an impressive student from India. I don't remember what his grades were or even what his professional experience was before entering the MBA program. All I know is that I wanted to help him. Why? Because he transformed our basic student-to-administrator relationship into something more meaningful. Before taking a holiday trip back to India, he stopped by my office to ask if I wanted him to bring me back anything. I'd never been to India, was flattered that he'd asked and felt a bit obliged to make a request. I casually suggested that he bring me back a small representation of a Hindu deity—assuming that he would forget. But he remembered to do it. I wasn't expecting it, and had actually forgotten my request when he handed me a little statue of Ganesh the next semester. The gift itself was of negligible financial value, and I'm sure it was available in any tourist souvenir shop. But his remembering my request and following through on his offer had a strong impact on our relationship, and on my motivation to help him in his job search. Six years later, Deep is a vice president at Bank of America and the small statue is still on my desk.

Credible, likable and helpful – Does this describe you?

Most religions have their "saints"—wise and magnanimous heroes who have given selflessly and significantly to all who ask and beyond. It's wonderful to have such people in the world. They're better than we are, and if we were all like them the world would be a better place. But at the moment, the rest of us are a bit less universally generous. In other words, we generally give on condition.[67] Ask yourself what conditions are likely to motivate you to help someone else? Unless you're a serial philanthropist, the individuals you help generally fall into four categories:

- those you like,

---

[67] Of course many of us do charitable work for the most needy in our society— as we should. You can consider yourself fortunate that you will not be needy enough to merit attention from this broad pool of societal generosity. Luckily for you, your U.S. employment needs are actually wants; but unluckily for you, people tend to satisfy the wants of others only on condition.

- those that are liked by someone you know and like,

- those who have helped you and

- those you think can help you later

In short, it's about being liked and being valuable. Making sure that you are both of these things not only ensures that people will be motivated to help you, but also, and equally important, that they will *remember* you when they have an opportunity to help you. Someone may want to help you, but if you don't pop into mind at the right moment, you miss out.

Being credible

Consultants have credibility because they are not dumb enough to work at your company.
—SCOTT ADAMS, creator of the office cartoon *Dilbert*

Credibility underlies all meaningful commitments and relationships. In building Power Ties, if you don't seem credible to the people you're connecting with, the relationship will go nowhere. Credibility means having people believe in you. Credibility signals to others that you are worth knowing, worth helping and worth keeping in touch with. How can you establish this trust? The first and most important step is to be real; be yourself.

Being yourself sounds easy (and perhaps a little cliché), but it isn't—particularly when building Power Ties for the first time. If you've never initiated an informational interview or participated in a professional networking activity, you may find yourself tempted to act as you think you "should" instead of being who you are. This is normal. In fact, your career services office probably has several script sheets you can reference to guide your conversation in new job search situations.

All but the most outgoing people hold tightly to their script and perform the role prescribed as they begin something new. Until you have enough experience to know how to handle a situation on your own terms, the script gives you security and confidence.

However, you should discard your script, and the temptation to "act," as soon as possible. Why? Because relationships are built on personalities, not formulas. The informational interview is a very powerful mechanism for building Power Ties, yet it is only a technique and won't do anything to set you apart from others who may be informational interviewing. Only your true personality or substance will differentiate you, complete with all your genuine interests and idiosyncrasies.[68]

---

[68] Tom Hopkins, the author of the classic book *How to Master the Art of Selling* stresses this same idea in sharing his selling techniques. "The power and the satisfaction of acquiring new knowledge and new skills lies in putting your mark on them." The techniques are important, but the true value comes from making them your own.

People can smell a script, and when they do, they lose patience and you lose credibility. Have you ever listened as a telemarketer reads from a prepared sales pitch? Ever sit through a PowerPoint presentation where the presenter just reads the bullets projected up on the slides? (I can read. Why do I need the presenter?) Scripts don't engage, they don't convince and they don't build rapport. With Power Ties, the same holds true. Most people you meet while informational interviewing will show patience and courtesy if they begin to sense that you're not being yourself, but you won't stand out as someone they should remember, and they won't be eager for any additional meetings. Someone who holds on to a script for too long will come across as phony, and phoniness = no credibility.

Your genuine personality and interests will shine more brightly than anything you can invent. Credibility and the strong Power Ties that result from it are established between people who are open and genuine with each other. Their authentic mutual interests fuel the mutual value they derive. Could this possibly happen if one participant pretended to be someone else?

Aside from just being yourself, here are some other ways to establish credibility:

- Do what you say you will do.[69]

---

[69] Call me a cynic, but following through on personal commitments has become a lost virtue—at least in the U.S. It has become more and more acceptable

- Never speak badly about a mutual acquaintance.[70]

- Refer your contact to another high quality person in your network. (more on this later)

- Get referred to your contact by someone he or she trusts.

- Ask a question that demonstrates special familiarity with your contact's area of expertise.

- Ask questions fueled by your natural curiosity—discard questions that will yield little that interests you.

Even when you're still using your script, don't worry so much about strictly following it. Jump in, be yourself and enjoy your journey and the wonderful people you're about to meet.

---

for people to forget about their commitments or simply to change their minds about them when they become inconvenient. In fact, it's likely that people you meet during informational interviews will assume that you WON'T honor your verbal commitments (unfortunately). The upside of this unfortunate situation is that it presents a huge (and easy) opportunity for you to differentiate yourself positively.

[70] I specify "mutual acquaintance" in order to differentiate from public figures. Disparaging someone you both know makes you look uncharitable and opportunistic. But people in the public arena may be excellent fodder for delicate critique. It's a good idea to avoid negativity in any early conversation with someone, but sharing your ideas on current events, sports or entertainment can be quite a good way to build rapport. You may stir controversy, but controversy, if handled with respect and dispassion, makes for scintillating conversation, and may showcase an important part of your personality.

Being likable

Good nature is more agreeable in conversation than wit,
and gives a certain air to the countenance
which is more amiable than beauty.
—JOSEPH ADDISON, English essayist

When I'm giving presentations on informational interviewing, I typically ask the audience if they've ever gone out of their way to help someone they didn't like. A few altruists tentatively raise their hands, to the amusement and skepticism of the rest of the group. Notwithstanding the saints among us—and God bless them—it feels much better to help people we care about than to help those we don't. Providing real help typically requires effort, and most people would rather reserve that effort to support people they think are worthy of it.

Likeability ranks second to credibility only because being likeable at the expense of your integrity isn't worth the price. You can't be liked by everyone, and better to be disliked for who you are than liked for who you are not. Once credibility has been established (and ideally, *while* credibility is being established), likeability is your next obvious objective.

So how can you be likable? That's up to you. But I have two recommendations—one enigmatic and one straightforward. First, the enigmatic: don't try too hard. Unless you're a gifted conversationalist, forget about "schmoozing,"[71] and forget about saying the perfect thing at the perfect moment. These things might happen, but usually not through trying. It's been my experience that a person's charm flows more freely from being relaxed.

Second, read Dale Carnegie's *How to Win Friends and Influence People*. I'm not going to waste your time by trying to add anything to this book's time-tested insights on making a positive impression. Having said that, I will highlight a few particularly critical but often overlooked points.

Energy is contagious

People love to meet other people who are loaded with positive energy. This is doubly true for overworked hiring managers. Be the fire in the furnace and you'll attract supporters and admirers. Keep away from anyone you encounter who tries to extinguish your fire. Your energy will be sapped.

Humor works

When I was first making presentations, someone said to me, "Once an audience laughs with you, they'll be on your side for the rest of your presentation."[72] How true this is. With laughter, drudgery becomes delight and hostility

---

[71] If you're not familiar with the term "to schmooze," it's a Yiddish slang verb often used in America to suggest making small talk, projecting social energy, and easily moving in and out of conversation with strangers. These are not bad skills to have, but relationship building doesn't depend on them.

[72] "Laughing with you…" is the operative phrase here. If an audience is laughing *at* you, the result could be quite different!

turns into support. If you have the gift of humor, use it liberally.

Genuine good nature trumps wit

If you're witty, that's great. Everyone loves hearing a clever comment at just the right time, or a piece of sharp or original insight. Witty people generally make good conversation and draw listeners. But, even though your wit can get you positive attention, it won't build enduring relationships on its own. If you're not witty, don't worry. Wit needs to come from a foundation of personal virtue to be trusted and liked over time. A good nature and a personal commitment to a set of values will demonstrate to others your reliability and your genuine concern for them. Good-natured people are likable and sought-out. They laugh often, they show interest in others, and they can be relied upon for help (see the next section).

--

I don't expect there will be much opposition to my recommendation to be likable. It is helpful to remind yourself of its importance by remembering how often you've made a true effort to help someone you didn't like. I'll bet you have trouble thinking of even one time. And even if you can, I'm confident you weren't eager to do it again. Keep this in mind as you do your outreach. Your chances of winning favor through being likeable are much higher than your chances of connecting with a saint.

Being helpful

Why do Power Ties work? Because people help each other. The third primary objective in building Power Ties is to deliver value—always. Giving generates goodwill, and goodwill is the currency of a powerful support group. What do you feel like doing when someone does something for you?

Later in the chapter, we'll talk very specifically about the value you can bring to a contact. But here's the challenge: Will you be able to see through your own needs in order to recognize the needs of others? While an informational interview is an opportunity for you to collect someone else's advice, it's also an opportunity to uncover how you might be of service. Listen to what your contact tells you. Concerns tend to be top of mind, and they often emerge in conversation of their own accord. Amid the information you collect will be revelations on challenges your contact is facing. If not, a well-crafted question about "current challenges" will generally elicit some very useful information. Make note of all that you learn and spend some time afterwards thinking about any positive impact you can make to help your contact, however small.

Another critical point: Don't keep score. Giving is profitable, but it is also good for its own sake. The world is full of people looking after their own interests only, and there is an expectation that you will do the same.

The extent to which you can demonstrate truly unselfish behavior to people who don't expect it is the extent to which you will win allies. Am I recommending you become one of the selfless saints I mentioned at the beginning of this section? Not really—although there are certainly less honorable ambitions. I'm recommending that if you find someone worthy of your help, you give it to him without expecting something in return.

Consider the people you know in your life. Who are the ones most cherished by others? Who are the people sought out for advice and referrals? Who are the people that everyone seems to know and wants to be around? These are the givers. They help other people through an authentic desire to make a difference and by dedicating time to creative problem solving. Connectors like this are easy to spot. For example, five minutes into a conversation with you, they'll think of someone you should meet and they'll make an immediate phone call to establish the connection. Or perhaps they'll remember an earlier conversation with you and a particular challenge you mentioned, and they'll send you an email the next day with a bit of information they thought you could use. They do all of this without keeping score, but they receive plentiful payback.

It's not my intention to preach ethics in this book; I want you to do what you need to do in order to get a job. But fortunately for those of us who enjoy networking, generosity and building Power Ties are complementary; people who receive tend to give back. Why? Because those who receive value those who give. You want to be valued? Be helpful.

Givers enjoy material success, but they also achieve deep personal fulfillment. They intuitively understand the rewards of being helpful, and they become the center of a Power Ties network. Your goal is to meet givers and become like them. If you're continually helping people who are worthy of your help (people who are credible, likeable and helpful themselves), you'll never have to worry about getting what you are owed.

Confidence – part of your reward

There's little debate that having and projecting confidence can have a huge impact on your success. Confidence makes you appear more convincing, more reliable, more valuable. The challenge is that genuine confidence is hard for most of us to summon without already having some experience and some taste of success.

So how can you build confidence as you begin your informational interviews—before you've tasted some success? There are several ways: reading this book, developing a strong outreach strategy and learning to tolerate risk will all help. But the most powerful way to feel and exude confidence is to focus on being valuable.

As we've just discussed, being credible, likeable and helpful makes you valuable to someone else. If you knew that you could positively affect someone's life, wouldn't that make you confident? Wouldn't you be eager to ask for someone's time if you knew you were worth it? You are!—for all the reasons already described.

I'm credible, likeable and helpful, but what do I have to offer?

If you think you're too small to have an impact, try going to bed with a mosquito.
—ANITA RODDICK, Founder of The Body Shop

While you're in a job search, it's important to have your accomplishments, references, objectives and personal sales pitches well organized and ready for distribution. But it's much more important that you create a receptive audience for your information by encouraging people to want to help you. There are many ways to deliver value to others, to demonstrate that you care about them and to initiate mutually beneficial relationships. However, not all these methods are readily apparent to the average international student.

International students always say to me, "Dan, I already know that it's important to help people while building a relationship. We all know that. But what do I have to give that a senior-level hiring manager—with many more contacts and years of experience than me—would ever want?" This is a common and legitimate concern. However, your potential value to a senior-level professional is beyond what you likely believe and can be delivered in ways you may not have considered. You represent immense potential value to a contact both as a professional and as a person.

Since informational interviewing is the method you're going to use to initiate Power Ties, we'll talk first about some very basic interpersonal tools at your disposal that can easily be used to establish rapport.

In an informational interview, you're going to feel the temptation to lead with your professional qualifications. Yes, you offer value to a hiring manager as a professional and you should be prepared to speak about it at the appropriate time. A manager needs to know that he's talking with someone who could be an asset as an employee or as a worthy referral to someone in his professional network. But don't think that your value begins or ends there. In fact, if it does, your Power Ties will be weak and you may not be remembered. Unless you have reason to believe that your contact has a specific interest in you as a professional at the very beginning of your relationship, your professional value is best shared later. Therefore, we're going to look at your potential value as a person first, and as a professional second. Are you ready to learn how valuable you are?

As a person

1. An interested ear

We all know that people love to speak about themselves. There is nothing more interesting to us than ourselves. This timeless truth is your reliable friend in initiating Power Ties. Your genuinely interested ear is your ticket to information and influence. We all have things that we are proud of and would love to share with others. Think of one of your most treasured accomplishments and imagine how eagerly you would embrace an opportunity to answer questions on every delicious detail. Your contacts are no different.

Many international students make the mistake of dominating a conversation with facts and figures about their own experience, interests and needs. This is understandable given the emphasis career services offices place on helping students perfect their "elevator pitch" and sell themselves. It's great to have your sales pitch at your finger tips. But it's best delivered at the request of someone who has already been primed to hear it. Have your questions ready and earn the right to share what you're proud of.

Remember that questions and showing genuine interest in the answers are the gifts you bring to others. Use them to calm any fears you may have of starting conversation with someone you don't know, or "prying" into someone's life. We've all got a story that we are eager to tell. Your challenge is to find out what it is in the person you're connecting with and give him or her the gift of an interested listener.

2. A chance to help someone (the "feel-good" factor)

Don't underestimate the impact you can have on someone by simply asking for advice. Implicit in such a request is an expression of admiration and respect, and most people will respond positively. Early in their careers, students don't fully appreciate a seasoned professional's need to mentor more junior people. Having an impact on others is something we all crave, and it grows as we accumulate more to share. Mentoring and teaching are part of what draws people to leadership and management in the first place. If you haven't already tasted the satisfaction that accompanies helping a junior colleague at work, you've likely experienced it in other ways—perhaps in representing your university to potential applicants.

Mentoring junior colleagues is personally rewarding and a sign of prestige. A tactful, respectful and genuine request for help from a more senior professional is a compliment, and you can generally expect gratitude and cooperation from the recipient.

3. Your personal network

> I not only use all the brains that I have,
> but all that I can borrow
> —WOODROW WILSON, 19th president of the United States

Everyone, no matter how accomplished, needs help with something. If you can find out what it is and deliver even the slightest level of assistance, you'll make a memorable first impression. Students are often intimidated by more senior people, but they forget that senior people face the same daily challenges that everyone else faces. For example, people in management tend to spend a lot of time at work, and often very little time anywhere else. They seem to be in constant need of home improvement contractors, housekeepers, babysitters, landscapers and myriad other reliable service providers that you could be referring to them. If you know people who provide services like these, do you think they'd appreciate getting new business? This is just an example, of course. Keep track of everyone you know and what they're good at so you can take advantage of an opportunity to make a difference. Connecting two people who need each other is how the strongest Power Ties are built.

In your meeting with a senior manager, you may also hear of critical job openings. If you think you're right for the position, be sure to mention your background (and other things I'll mention soon). If you're not right for the role, explore your own network to see if you know someone who is. Do you think doing this will differentiate you from your competition? Guaranteed! What do you think will happen if you do this twice, or three times? Do you think people will want to be in your network? Wouldn't it be great to have people reaching out to you because of who *you* know? Develop a reputation as a connector and you will find a downhill path to success.

4. Interesting ideas, perspectives, knowledge

To move others, you have to speak beyond yourself.
—KEITH FERRAZZI, author of *Never Eat Alone*.

While we're listing what you have to offer, let's not forget the obvious: interesting information. You need to have something interesting to say or talk about. You need a point of view, a story to tell, something memorable and identifiable with you. All people love to talk about themselves, but the most interesting and sustainable conversation grows from ideas—mostly in a field of common interest among the participants. A conversation between two astronomers debating a piece of research on pulsars will be much more engaging to both of them than if one of them droned on about his grandmother's collection of porcelain bananas. Think about the people you're connecting with. What's likely to be of interest to them—and to you? What do you know about that topic?

I'm not suggesting that facts and figures are your ticket to scintillating conversation. Too much data is boring, and reciting it risks appearing pedantic. Instead, ask a simple question: "What do you think about...?" Such questions are a powerful way to initiate meaningful and enjoyable idea-based conversation because they elicit something interesting that you can react to—a point of view. While you want to avoid anything overly controversial, you'll find that people are far more interested in what you *think* than what you know. The best of both worlds is to have a well thought-out position based on knowledge. You'll be able to engage your target audience and look like an insider.

How do you do this?

- Keep track of interesting bits of information: ones that make you think.

- Keep track of questions that pop into your head in the middle of the day that can only be answered by people with particular expertise. When you find those people (and you will eventually) and ask your questions, you'll impress them with your insight (and you'll get an informed answer!).

- Keep track of interesting ideas you've heard during other conversations—ideas from people who may be recognized in your field, and which might be of interest to others.

- Read Chapter 22 of Keith Ferazzi's *Never Eat Alone* entitled "Be Interesting." The entire book is powerful reading, but Chapter 22 gives potent suggestions on bringing subject-matter value to a conversation.

As a professional

Once you've considered giving your contact a reason to care about you as a person, it's appropriate to think about presenting your value as a professional. You've got refined skills, diverse work experiences, subject-related interests and a respected education: all the things you're most eager to talk about—and all the things every *other* job seeker is eager to talk about. Your professional background may be special enough to get someone's attention on its own, but why take that risk? The true key here is differentiation. Does your contact believe that there are a thousand other people like you running around looking for work? If so, why should she refer you for a friend's open position if she thinks her friend would have no problem finding someone like you on her own?

Average salespeople adequately demonstrate that their product can do the job, but great sales people work to differentiate their product from the competition. Here's where your "international student" status becomes an asset to the right hiring manager. The most effective international student job seekers I've observed have gotten themselves in front of hiring managers who would appreciate not just their professional skills, but the unique offerings derived from their international status.

What would such a hiring manager look like, you ask? Good question; and you'll need to figure it out based on your background and professional objectives. But here are a few hiring manager characteristics that are likely to help your cause. Move to the top of your priority list any hiring manager who:

- Is from a country outside of the U.S., or better yet, from your country

- Manages people in other countries

- Manages people with work visas

- Is currently on a work visa

- Sells to international markets

- Speaks another language

- Travels frequently for work, or

- Went to school outside of his native country.

Now, we move on to what you can offer a manager as a professional.

1. International perspective

It's a global economy, right? Despite the fact that so many American companies are now global, they can be quite short on international perspective. U.S. firms need employees familiar with how business is done in other parts of the world, and local professional networks to lubricate that business. You bring both of these assets, and you should practice articulating their value to a hiring manager. Your career services office can help you craft and practice delivering a compelling proposition.

2. Language skills

Perhaps the most mono-lingual animal on the planet is the non-immigrant American. In my opinion, foreign language education in the U.S. is very poor. Why? Because Americans don't value speaking other languages as much as their counterparts around the world. English being everywhere, there's little incentive for many Americans to master another language. But as huge new markets of non-English-speaking consumers open up around the world (and within the U.S.), your language skills are a powerful and easily-sold advantage. Leverage them.

As you tout your multiple language skills, make it clear beyond question to your listener that English is one of your strengths. A mastery of English, the international business language, is essential for any job in the United States that involves advocating ideas, developing strategy and building relationships. What good is it to learn how to sell yourself if you don't possess the language skills to make yourself clearly understood in the country where you want to work? If you notice your American friends concentrating a little too hard when you speak, it might be an indication that your English could use improvement. Learn English well—including the accent—and you will do well.[73]

I've conducted interviews in person and over the phone where I couldn't really understand what the candidate was saying. What a waste of time for both of us! After making a couple of polite requests for a candidate to repeat himself, I would end the conversation and move on if things didn't improve. Even if you're seeking one of the few remaining careers that will keep you cloistered in a cube with near-zero human contact, you still need strong enough English skills to get the

---

[73] Many students overlook accent training. They don't realize that it doesn't matter if your grammar is flawless if no one can understand what you're saying. When I was a student in France, it was painful to try to imitate the French accent. I felt uncomfortable because the sounds I was making were strange to my ears. Those sounds, however, were music to the ears of the French. OK, maybe I'm overstating things! Just don't forget that mastering the accent is a critical part of learning a language; after all, the only point of speaking in the first place is to be understood!

job in the first place. And that means being able to explain yourself with energy and clarity to an English-speaking hiring manager.

Once you've mastered English, you've taken a significant step in differentiating yourself—not only from other international students whose English may be weak, but also from the mono-linguist Americans. Multiple language skills translate into value for many hiring managers.

3. Desire

I've encountered scores of international students looking for work (and sponsorship). Their general enthusiasm for working in the States and willingness to go the extra distance have made them stand out from the typical applicant. In a world where job seekers act increasingly aloof and entitled, an engaged candidate makes a strong positive impression. Let your enthusiasm for finding a career in the U.S. motivate you to be positive, energetic and eager. These are all qualities that impress people—especially a hiring manager who has a lot of work to do and not enough eager employees to help him.

Take care to purposefully translate your enthusiasm for working in the States into enthusiasm for a specific career path or company. In other words, make sure your contact believes that you are interested in a particular career path first and U.S. work sponsorship second. As I mentioned earlier, it's been my experience that international students wear their need for sponsorship too obviously. While managers will go to great lengths to refer, acquire and satisfy a candidate who projects enthusiasm, they are quick to close the door on anyone who exhibits desperation. Avoid making comments like "I'm willing to do anything."[74]

Remember the rules of selling: people buy when they see a solution to their problem. Your need for visa sponsorship is your problem, not the manager's. Hiring managers care about producing quality work on time. They're not looking for someone to do "anything." If someone you are informational interviewing needs to hire, she needs help with something specific. Therefore, let your desire for sponsorship motivate you, but let the desires of the manager guide how you articulate your value. This is the best way to create a match that will satisfy the desires of both of you.

4. Diversity (but beware!)

When I was recruiting for Monster, I was often approached by non-white international students who pitched themselves as diverse candidates. Although some of your advisors are likely to disagree with me on this point, I believe the risks in making a diversity

---

[74] Don't laugh. I've heard this comment surprisingly often. Remarks of desperation don't help you.

pitch outweigh the potential benefits. Let me explain.

Mentioning diversity, a very hot topic in American recruiting, is certainly a good way to get someone's attention. U.S. firms have clearly put their resources behind diversity initiatives, and some recruiters get bonus dollars for every "diverse" candidate they hire. So what's the risk of using diversity as a way to pitch your value? You'll find that many people do not consider international students to be diverse hires— regardless of where they're from. Right or wrong, your lack of work authorization might remove you from what the company considers to be the pool of legitimate "diverse" candidates. Therefore, raising the issue may cause contention.

In addition, most diverse American candidates don't openly try to lever their diversity in order to advance their careers. If you do, you run the risk of doing one of two counterproductive things: first, directing attention away from the primary reason why someone should hire you (your ability to do a job very well), or second, appearing manipulative. Diversity means different things to different people: diversity of race, gender, perspective, sexual orientation, work experience, national origin, etc. But there is utter uniformity in that no one involved in hiring wants to be thought of as insensitive to diversity. If you mention it, you risk provoking differences in opinion on what it means.

And it's counterproductive to rouse the natural defensiveness many Americans feel regarding this topic.

Forgo the awkwardness of pointing out the obvious (i.e., that you aren't white) or making potentially false presumptions (i.e., that you fit that company's definition of "diverse") and let the person you're connecting with make his or her own judgments. While it's quite possible you may benefit from a company's commitment to building a diverse workforce, there is little to be gained by directly calling attention to the issue.

What are your motives?

Build it before you need it

Harvey McKay—an icon of business self-help and selling—wrote a book on professional networking called *Dig Your Well Before You're Thirsty*. The title implies that you must build your network before you need it. If you're exuding need in your first meeting with someone, you can be sure that person will smell your self-interest and recoil. People want to help, but they don't like to feel used and they often try to avoid the pressure associated with making commitments.

Let's imagine that you've made the mistake of waiting until April to begin building Power Ties for your job search.

You've wasted months submitting résumés on the job boards and hoping you'll be found. It hasn't worked, and you're feeling intense pressure to find a U.S. job before graduation.[75] So far, with a quick change in tactics, you've managed to schedule one informational interview with an alumnus from your school. As you walk in to shake hands with your contact, what do you think he or she can see written all over your face? You'll be wearing your urgent need for a job like a cheap suit, and you will have trouble disguising it. You've waited too long to dig your well. Your contact will sense your irrepressible urgency, feel pressure, and withdraw.

To receive maximum benefit, build your network before you need it. Do yourself the favor of building Power Ties from a position of strength, not from a position of desperation. Only then will you be able to focus on giving instead of extracting. Only then will you have the patience and the confidence to build the relationships required for mutual benefit.

You can't have genuine confidence if you don't feel right about what you're doing. Don't confuse being strategic with being manipulative.

---

[75] In my experience this unfortunately describes the approach of about half of all international students. I'm continually amazed how many business students—people who are normally driven, competitive and innovative—embrace the hopelessly passive model of job boards. The only explanation I can think of is that these students haven't yet been taught a better way. After reading this far, you no longer have that excuse. If it's April, and this describes you, all is not lost! You're under more time pressure to get your Power Ties network growing, but with some extra effort, you can do it. Start by committing to yourself that you will arrange at least two informational interviews a week.

A word about calculation

There is a slippery component of the Power Ties mindset that needs to be addressed. Does all of this seem obnoxiously self-serving? Does building Power Ties feel like manipulating people to get them to help you? Here are some familiar comments of skepticism that I've heard in my career: "I'm targeting people that I want to know because I think they can get me something that I want. I'm putting them on a list, I'm tracking them down to get their time, and I'm trying to make myself important to them so that they are likely to help me. I don't really care about these people, do I? It's not like I'm spending time with them because I value them as people. I feel fake because I'm pretending to care when I really don't. I hate this networking stuff."

You could fall into this dangerous mindset if you don't spend time at the outset thinking about your value and committing yourself to being helpful whenever you can. No one can be a good networker if he feels that he's using people. People who are unfamiliar with the give-and-take of networking (such as students who come from countries where building a professional network is less common) often fall into this trap. If you aren't helpful to others in some way, however small, you won't feel good about what you're doing, and you likely won't receive much help!

Before you dive into building Power Ties, ask yourself these basic questions and be honest with yourself. Do you enjoy helping other people? Are relationships important to you? Do you believe in the value of teamwork? If the answer to these questions is "no," you may want to reconsider going into a business career. If the answer is "yes," then you're ready to make some calls, schedule some meetings, and begin to participate in relationship-based business. In *The One Minute Salesperson*, Spencer Johnson coaches sales people to consider the following truth: "I get what I want when I help enough other people get what they want."

We've just spent this chapter reviewing the ways that you can add value to someone else's life. Take these ideas to heart, commit yourself to being helpful whenever you can and you won't feel that you are using people. Although we have spent time in this book "calculating" how to build a network of Power Ties that is helpful to you in your life, the value you get from it will not come at someone else's expense—just the opposite. If you follow my advice, people who are a part of your network will benefit from knowing you; they will want to help you. If they don't, then you won't be building Power Ties.

Conclusion

The message is simple, really: deliver value whenever you can. Never stop evaluating yourself from an outside perspective. Would *you* return your phone calls? Would *you* take time out of your busy day to meet with you? Would *you* refer you to your friends? The answers to these questions must be "yes" for you to have success building Power Ties. And if you concern yourself with delivering value to others first, it will be your name that comes up when an open position emerges in the hidden job market. You will be the one invited to come in to interview before an open position is known to your competition or any other potential applicants. You will enter the interview with one and possibly multiple endorsements. And you will be hired by people powerful enough to get you an H-1B visa.

Imagine yourself with a fabulous U.S. job and a deep network of supporters to help you be successful. Sounds good, doesn't it?

Conclusion
What will you do now?

When you play it too safe, you're taking the biggest risk of your life. Time is the only wealth we're given.
—BARBARA SHER, best-selling author of *Wishcraft*

You've just been introduced to the Power Ties system. Before you begin to feel overwhelmed by all of the moving pieces, remember that you don't need to get every step of the process right all of the time to be successful. While putting it all together perfectly is the goal, perfection is rarely achievable. But there is plenty of value to be enjoyed even if you're only able to do some of the things well. *Taking action and making improvements is most important.*

You might be thinking that the Power Ties system makes sense. You might also be thinking that it sounds like a lot of work. You'd be right on both points. Building enduring Power Ties is perhaps the most challenging activity that you'll encounter as a professional. Not because meeting people is difficult, but because good relationship building takes practice and skill. A good networker needs persistence in executing a vision, a tolerance for risk, effective communication skills, an attentive ear to other people's needs and an ability to inspire others to action. These traits are all critical to building Power Ties, but aren't they also the traits of effective leadership? Is mastering these things not the logical conclusion of all the training you've just received in school?

Executives spend their time building teams and inspiring action. They take risks and overcome setbacks. American business schools claim to be creating leaders, yet many schools focus heavily on building hard skills and neglect the softer skills of leadership. As you build Power Ties in pursuit of a job, you'll accomplish several things.

First, you'll overcome whatever fear you might have of reaching out to people you don't know. Making connections with new people, no matter how intimidating, is a basic business skill that becomes even more critical as you climb the corporate ladder.

Second, you'll learn what things inspire people to action. I've already mentioned being credible, likeable and helpful. You'll discover through practice the techniques that will work for you in accomplishing these things. You'll use these tactics throughout your professional life—from moving to new jobs, to building your team of employees, to generating and solidifying client relationships.

Third, you'll find a job in the U.S. and likely lay the

groundwork for job security for many years to come. Job security in the United States doesn't come from loyalty to a company but from loyalty to a personal and professional network. If you understand this, you will have a successful career in the United States and likely wherever your professional life may take you.

Fourth, you'll make friends. Is there anything more important?

Having read this far, you might wonder if there is an easier way. Are Power Ties worth the planning, the extra effort, the discomfort? Maybe you've had some friends who went through traditional campus recruiting activities and found a job. Maybe they were good and maybe they were lucky. Before you decide that you're going to follow in their footsteps, you should ask yourself these questions:

- Has my success in life come from hoping for things to happen, or from taking control and making them happen?

- In a business world flooded with new graduates, what will I do to differentiate myself?

- Am I willing to step outside my comfort zone to learn, grow and create opportunity? Not many people are, and therein lies your chance to be extraordinary.

You've already displayed uncommon courage, given that you're out of your home country, likely studying in a non-native language, and about to embark on a job search in a different culture. You're taking bold steps to improve your career, and you deserve the rewards for the risks you have taken. A Power Ties network, and the access it will provide you to jobs, resources and support over your lifetime, will be the most valuable asset you bring with you as you begin your career. The sooner you start creating it, the better.

About the author

Over the past twelve years, Dan Beaudry has been on all sides of recruiting: from hiring manager to candidate counselor to third-party recruiter. He is experienced enough to be intimately familiar with the recruiting world, yet young enough to remember what it's like to be an international student. He holds a BA from Vanderbilt University, an MA in International Relations from Boston University, and language certifications from La Sorbonne in Paris.

Dan lives in Boston with his wife, Elena (who is from Spain, and has been given more advice on her U.S. job search than she ever asked for!)

Made in the USA
Lexington, KY
04 October 2015